THE GRAND CANYON,
EVOLUTION,
AND
INTELLIGENT DESIGN

THE GRAND CANYON, EVOLUTION, AND INTELLIGENT DESIGN

DR. RICHARD S. BEAL, JR.

Lighthouse
eBooks

THE GRAND CANYON, EVOLUTION, AND INTELLIGENT DESIGN

Copyright © by Richard S. Beal, Jr., 2007

The following Bible translations are used for quotation. Copyright is acknowledged and used with permission:

Published by
Lighthouse Christian Publishing
SAN 257-4330
5531 Dufferin Drive
Savage, Minnesota, 55378
United States of America

www.lighthouseebooks.com
www.lighthousechristianpublishing.com

ABOUT THE AUTHOR

Richard S. Beal, Jr. earned his B. S. degree with a major in Zoology at the University of Arizona and his Ph. D. degree in Entomology at the University of California, Berkeley. His career includes teaching Systematic Theology at Denver Seminary, employment as a research entomologist by the U. S. Department of Agriculture and stationed at the Smithsonian Institution, serving as an associate professor of zoology at Arizona State University and as a professor of zoology and Dean of the Graduate College at Northern Arizona University. Currently he and his wife live in Prescott, Arizona, where he teaches an adult Bible class at the First Baptist Church.

To my wife Evorine

CONTENTS

ABBREVIATIONS
NAB: New American Bible
NASB: New American Standard Bible
NIV: New International Version
NRSV: New Revised Standard Version

PREFACE

Readers should be alerted to a conscious bias of mine. I am an evangelical Christian committed to the doctrine of Biblical inerrancy, and I write from such a point of view. I belong to what the famous biologist Sir Gavin de Beer sneeringly termed, "fundamentalist sects, which accept a literal interpretation of the Bible." I doubt that de Beer knew what a literal interpretation of the Bible amounts to, or ought to amount to. For that matter, many earnest Christians give little thought to how the Bible should be interpreted.

Growing up in the family of a vigorous and highly esteemed fundamentalist Baptist pastor, I was firmly convinced that biological evolution represents the pinnacle of unbelief. I was equally certain that no interpretation of Genesis 1 could be allowed except the ruin and reconstruction interpretation, the one found in the *Scofield Reference Bible*. In the 1920s and '30s my father was heavily involved in his own creation-evolution controversy with some professors at the University of Arizona and several liberal Tucson clergymen.[1] Many of the leading creationists of those years were visitors in our home, one of whom was the Presbyterian clergyman Dr. Harry Rimmer. This gentleman, a prolific creationist author, took a personal interest in me, greatly encouraging my own interest in science. His particular influence, together with my father's convictions, stayed with me through college, through some years in seminary, through two pastorates, and into graduate work in entomology at the University of California, Berkeley. It was impossible for me to entertain any other interpretation of the Bible or even tentatively question the doctrine of instantaneous creation by divine commands.

Dr. Edward A. Steinhaus was one of the towering intellectuals for whom Berkeley was so famous. He was the father of the science of insect pathology, and one of the pioneers in developing biological control of insect pests. I had not had him for a class and scarcely knew him, although I had met him at the departmental, Friday afternoon, faculty/graduate-student teas. One day he sent word that I was to see him in his office. After short pleasantries he said, "I understand you have been engaging in some heated discussions on evolution with some of the other students." He then demanded, "Is that true?"

Awaiting some atheistic tirade, I weakly admitted it was so. To my astonishment, that eminent scientist reached to a bookshelf next to his desk, took down a well-worn copy of the Bible, opened to the Book of Genesis, and responded, "Let's see what the Scriptures have to say." The years have now erased the rest of our conversation. I wish I could recall every word. Whatever that great and devout man said, his reverence for the Scriptures and his ability to find a personal synthesis of science and faith broke the chains that entangled my vision. He encouraged my faith, yet at the same time enabled me to consider objectively the data both of the Biblical text and of science.

Will my personal quest following that conversation, as I attempt to relate a small part of my findings, help others look at the questions fairly and openly? If so, my efforts in writing this book will have been justified.

I sympathize most with people for whom the problems of evolution and creation are not rational or objective, but heartfelt. A student commented to me, "No matter what I read or what anyone says to me, I simply cannot be convinced that my ancestors were monkey-like animals." Nor am I trying to compel anyone to think as much. Rather, I invite people who have strong emotions on creationist doctrine, as well as those who have intellectual questions, to look fairly at all sides of the question. I know that for many Christians, the term evolution itself is anathema. I only hope readers will not be deterred by my use of the word but will follow the concepts I develop.

This is primarily for the benefit of the Christian in the pew, the Sunday school teacher, the clergyman, and Christian college students who have a genuine desire for a clear understanding of the issues, and who want to find some satisfactory answers. It is for the parents of questioning young people. In any event, I shall have met my objectives, first, if I can help sincere Christian people keep an open mind on the questions. Second, if I can dissuade my brothers and sisters from focusing on tangential issues. What truly matters is not my view or some other view of God's choice of a creative method, but what happened at Calvary and the meaning of the empty tomb!

What follows is a reduced version of an earlier, rather large manuscript. That manuscript was read by a number of reviewers, and individual chapters were read by others. I cannot thank everyone who critically read one of those individual chapters, for some would be surprised to find what they read completely missing in this book. I do offer my deepest appreciation to those who have read separate chapters, or all of my various drafts, and have offered critical and helpful comments. Not all reviewers by any means have agreed with my conclusions. A few have views turned 180° from mine. Yet all have had a share in shaping my thinking as well as helping me with the expression of my ideas. Within their respective fields each has contributed information out of stores of knowledge far richer than mine, or has helpfully exposed some obscure writing. I must admit that I have stubbornly rejected a few corrections from some excellent scholars, so if there are errors the responsibility is wholly mine. Those I especially thank are David P. Beal, Stanley S. Beus, Richard H. Bube, Archie Dickey, Pete Lupescu, Glenn R. Morton, Robert O'Connell, Joe Palmer, Peter W. Price, Dwight M. Slater, Rosemary Snellman, Barry

C. Willis, and Gerald Winkleman. I especially thank Robert A. Pyne of Dallas Theological Seminary not only for a helpful reading of the manuscript but for suggesting some valuable additional literature and for sharing some of his unpublished lecture notes. I thank Kurt P. Wise, Glenn R. Morton, and George F. Howe for calling my attention to some literature sources that I had missed. Keith B. Miller of the Department of Geology of Kansas State University graciously sent me a prepublication draft of an article of his, for which I extend my thanks. Frank R. Ames kindly commented on a chapter and suggested some valuable references, for which I am grateful. I thank George E. Webb for sending me a reprint of his article on Tucson's evolution debate. I thank the Reverend M. B. Roberts of Chirk, Wrexham, Wales, for sending me a draft of his paper on the history of the creation/science conflict. I thank John R. Meyer of the Creation Research Society for allowing me the privilege of using the library at the Van Andel Research Center. I thank Rudy Baranko for some valuable computer assistance. I wish especially to express my appreciation to my editor, Chris Wright of Bristol, U.K., for his excellent and patient help in bringing the book to completion.

All Biblical quotations are from the *New American Standard Bible*, except as otherwise noted.

My efforts and the contributions of my reviewers will have been eminently worthwhile if my readers will have their minds directed away from fruitless controversies, and directed toward the true elegance eof God's Word – and above all to the radiant beauty of the eternal Lord of Life Himself.

CHAPTER 1

INTRODUCTION

Visitors to the Grand Canyon National Park since the middle of 2003 may have purchased a book entitled, *Grand Canyon, a Different View*, written and compiled by Tom Vail.[2] It includes short essays by a number of Bible-believing Christians, most of whom have doctoral degrees in some field of science or engineering. It is professionally produced and filled with splendid, colored photographs of the canyon, its rock formations, plants and animals. The purpose of the book is to demonstrate the literal veracity of the creation accounts of the Bible, and the utter bankruptcy of the evolutionary theory of creation. By a literal interpretation of the Bible, *Grand Canyon, a Different View* tries to demonstrate that the canyon was formed from its basement rocks to the top within the last 10,000 or so years. Its target audience is Christians, but the text obviously enough hopes to convince unbelievers as well.

Is the concept of a roughly 10,000 year-old earth the peculiar notion of a small, aberrant offshoot of fundamentalist Christians? Not at all. Without question, it is the firm belief of a quite large and respectable number of Christians, primarily those in the United States calling themselves evangelicals.

In stark contrast, the standard account for the formation of the Grand Canyon of the Colorado holds that the oldest rocks at the bottom were formed well over 700 million years ago, and that the succeeding layers were deposited over the millions of years that followed. Most certainly they were not formed within a bare ten thousand years. Added to this is the doctrine that the animals and plants entombed as fossils in the rocks were branches of a gradually descending tree of life. The canyon fossils are believed to harmonize with the widely-accepted tenet of organic evolution. This account is explained in a number of popularly-written books offered for sale in Grand Canyon bookstores, as well as in textbooks of geology.

In general, organic evolution is the concept that all life has had a common ancestry. Should this be true, sometime in the distant past such remarkably diverse things as tuberculosis bacilli, mushrooms, cottonwood trees, mosquitoes, snapping turtles, woodpeckers, mountain lions, chimpanzees and humans had a common ancestor. They and all other forms of life descended by slow, gradual, incremental steps from this one ancestor.

The question follows, how can intelligent, educated people hold two such totally incompatible views of the origin of this magnificent, awe-inspiring canyon and its remnants of life? Is it simply that some believe and others deny the Bible and the God it presents?

True, many professional geologists and biologists (the people responsible for the standard view of the canyon) have little use for God. Likely he doesn't exist. A few among these scientists surmise that a supernatural power might lurk somewhere in the universe. After all, why is there something instead of nothing? So if God does exist, he possibly had something to do with igniting the Big Bang – little more. The Big Bang and philosophical speculation aside, most biologists are firmly convinced that modern science demonstrates the total absence of God in the origin and history of life. Furthermore, God has nothing to do with what is happening to living things today. Most certainly, in no demonstrable way is he stirring the pot of human affairs.

Perhaps we can understand why most biologists and geologists find no evidence of a believable God, not when we see the world the way they do. The physical world operates predictably on the basis of physical laws. If someone is struck fatally by lightning, sad friends can only murmur, "What bad luck to be standing in the wrong place." Few people believe it was God's doing. It was the coming together of identifiable physical processes that happened to catch the poor blighter unawares. Was oil found on the frozen shores of northern Alaska? God didn't put it there to rescue the fortunes of wastrel, car-loving Americans. Geological events following physical laws put it there. Petroleum geologists, knowledgeable of the laws, had the ingenuity to discover it. At one time, vivid displays of the aurora borealis, the dancing northern lights, struck fear into people. The displays were often considered divine omens of impending battles. It took scientists several hundred years to discover the cause, but now most everyone knows the earth acts as a gigantic magnet, guiding particles from the sun into the earth's upper atmosphere. Here the particles collide with air molecules and produce light. The laws of physics explain what happens, just as they explain other physical events in our world.

Until Charles Darwin meditated on and published what he observed traveling around South America as a naturalist aboard the H. M. S. Beagle (1831-1836), biologists doubted the existence of God. They were frustrated in their disbelief, for they had no answers to Christian apologists who demanded an explanation for the remarkable intricacies of such things as the human eye, feathers of birds, exquisite flowers of orchids. Darwin found the answers. It wasn't because he thought of the theory of evolution, for he didn't. Jean Baptiste de Lamarck proposed a theory of evolution a generation earlier. In fact, Darwin's own grandfather Erasmus Darwin was an evolutionist. What Charles did was put together a coherent, totally natural explanation to account for evolution. He showed, at least to the satisfaction of thousands of biologists, that the complexity of life can neatly be explained by laws as reasonable as those that govern the physical world.3 Collectively, the laws are termed natural selection.

In the years since Darwin, his principles of natural selection have repeatedly been observed in operation. The concept of natural selection has been powerfully reinforced by connecting it with the laws of genetics and an understanding of the mechanisms of the cell. Darwin's principles of natural selection failed to put God to death; they simply banished him to a remote corner.

If everything obeys clearly ascertainable laws, where is God? Small wonder biologists and geologists marvel when they encounter a reputable biologist or geologist so regressive as to believe in the God of the Bible. Small wonder there is such pronounced opposition to the notion of intelligent design, the concept that God or some super being was responsible for the complexity of life. Yet surprisingly enough, there are a few authentic biologists and geologists who actually do subscribe to such a God and who believe God was involved in the design of living things. Although they swim against the tide, there are those for whom the *ipsissima verba* of Scripture speak truth and who are firmly convinced they have found their way through the thorny tangles of science and Biblical faith.

What rationale can anyone in this scientifically enlightened age find for believing in the God of the Bible? Can a competent scientist discover a reasonable excuse? Or is belief in the God of the Bible nothing more than intellectual backwardness?

Whether I can lay claim to being a truly competent scientist, others will have to judge. In any event, I am a published biologist and spent much of my adult life as a professor of zoology at two different state universities. I firmly believe in the personal, all-knowing, all-powerful, all-present, eternally-existing, righteous yet loving God revealed in the Bible. I do not believe in him because science has somehow proven his existence. Nor do I believe because science has presumably demonstrated the reliability of the Bible. Primarily I believe because I have found God in the person and witness of Jesus Christ. Then I believe in him because I have discovered him working through my most intimate, personal circumstances. This discovery came neither through a mind-boggling epiphany nor a fervid struggle of soul. Rather it grew as I reflected on the numerous and multifaceted evidences of God's grace that I have observed over the many years of my life.

The Bible presented Jesus Christ to me. But is the Bible dependable? Can it be trusted? The numerous miracles of the Bible, including the miracles recorded of Christ, seem wholly unreasonable because they are so outrageously improbable and so inexplicable to anyone knowing elementary principles of science. Similarly, the Biblical accounts of creation seem to stand in intractable contrast to so much that is known of biology and geology. These two areas, creation and accounts of the miraculous, likely more than any others, keep Christians and secular scientists worlds apart.

I am fully convinced there is a beautiful harmony between Biblical faith and valid science, including science that measures the age of Grand Canyon rocks in hundreds of millions instead of thousands of years.[4] Further, the basic elements of that harmony are reasonable and easily understood. Unfortunately, the basic elements are muddied by scientists who are unable or unwilling to distinguish between valid science and their metaphysical prejudices. On the other side, the elements of the harmony are equally muddied by sincere Christians seeking to defend certain interpretations of Biblical creation accounts, even though the interpretations are unwarranted and altogether improbable.

A number of Christian apologists have wrestled with the question of Biblical miracles. Did they really occur? Were they suspensions of the laws of nature, or were they divine utilization of mysterious natural laws not yet understood or discovered? Did something like miracles occur but the observers superstitiously overlooked some perfectly natural explanations? Or were the miracles the products of repeated retelling of stories, the stories having been unconsciously enlarged with each retelling? Each possibility has its advocates. At this point, I simply want to affirm my own belief in the authenticity of Biblical miracles. I believe each has an explanation that does no violence to canons of science, but the canons of science, that is, the laws of nature, are surface appearances of a deeper reality. This is a matter to be discussed toward the end of the book. The contentious issue of God's actions in creation and what he did to produce the Grand Canyon and marvelous complexities of life on earth need to come first.

To examine the question, we need to consider what the Bible actually teaches about creation (chapters 2-4). Next we need to see what God has manifestly said in the world he has created (chapters 5, 6). Finally we need to discover whether Biblical teaching about the nature and character of God can bring each facet into clear focus (chapter 7). But first, how have others resolved the seeming discrepancies between God's revelation and science?

Christian proposals to explain how creation may have occurred can be sorted into five broad categories. At this stage I am not considering possible ways of interpreting the first chapters of the book of Genesis, which is a separate but not unimportant question. Rather, I need to describe how the origin of life and mankind is accounted for by those unwilling to abandon faith in a personal, sovereign, and omnipotent God. The following are major theories advanced by

Christian thinkers who have grappled with issues of creation and evolution.

Young-earth Creationism

Until the beginning of the sixteenth century, few Christian thinkers questioned the belief that God created the world in six literal days and that the remains of plant and animal life found in the rocks were any other than organisms overcome by the flood of Noah. Leonardo da Vinci (1452-1519) was one of the first to question that belief, for he found marine shells on high mountains lying in positions incompatible with deposition by turbulent waters of a flood. Nevertheless, Christians were generally untroubled by the received doctrine. Archbishop James Ussher (1581-1656) formalized the doctrine by specifying that the world was created in 4004 B.C. followed by a "chaos" lasting only twelve hours, then creation within six days. The chaos was expressed by the words in Genesis 1:2, "without form and void." Yet scientifically inclined Christians during the 17th Century speculated that the chaos may have lasted significantly longer. This is reflected in an Anglican Bible commentary by Patrick, Willoughby, and Lowth published in 1694, which explained that the chaos might have lasted "a great while." During the following century, theologians and Biblical commentators for the most part adopted a "chaos-restitution" explanation of creation, many being vague about the duration of the chaos but considering it of some length and not part of the first day.[5] Still there continued to be commentators up through the nineteenth century who held that all creation took place within six literal days, the chaos being part of the first day.

The common young-earth version, currently held by so many evangelical Christians in America, places the chaos within the first day and defends a creation of the world and all its inhabitants within a literal week of time. Dinosaurs and other extinct animals and plants, large and small, were created the same week as Adam and Eve. These multiplied and lived contemporaneously with mankind. Prior to the flood of Noah there were few if any sedimentary rocks, and the landscape was relatively flat. The waters of the Biblical flood had two sources, a canopy of vapor above the earth and great reservoirs of water below the crust.[6] The canopy gave way and the reservoirs broke open in enormous fountains. As the flood waters swept over the earth, they formed most of the sedimentary rocks found in the world today, the sandstones, the limestones, the shales and the mudstones. These are rocks with fossil remains of corals, shellfish, arthropods, fish, amphibians, reptiles, birds, mammals, petrified forests, and of course, the great coal seams. After the flood, the crust sank in places to accommodate the waters in the now greatly deepened oceans. At the same time there were violent earth movements and volcanic eruptions that raised the mountains to their present heights.

Young-earth proponents also hold that all terrestrial animal life, including numerous now-extinct forms, was saved on Noah's ark. Extinct terrestrial invertebrates, reptiles, birds and mammals were initially saved, but died out sometime later, being unable to tolerate the changed environment of the earth following the flood.[7]

It may be just as useful to term this the *flood geology view*, since it requires the creation of such prehistoric animals as the dinosaurs within the same week as mankind, concludes that most of the fossils found in the rocks were entombed by the flood, and argues that most extinct species actually became extinct sometime after the flood. This doctrine is expounded in a plethora of books for sale in Christian bookstores everywhere.[8]

Reconstruction Creationism

The *Scofield Reference Bible*, first published in 1909 by Oxford University Press and updated and republished a number of times since, greatly impacted the Biblical understanding of American evangelicals. Probably from the time of its publication until about 1961, a large majority of evangelicals accepted the interpretation of Genesis 1 proposed in its notes. The view received some previous popularity through the book by G. H. Pember, *Earth's Earliest Ages*, first published in 1876. The view is more than an interpretation of Genesis 1. It represents an effort to square Genesis with geological evidence for a great age of the earth and for ancient animal and plant life.

The view proposes an initial creation some indefinitely great time prior to the six creative days of Genesis. Genesis 1:1: "In the beginning God created the heavens and the earth," is considered to be a statement of God's initial creation of the world in the remote past. The myriad prehistoric species of animals and plants found as fossils were all part of this original creation. For some reason – usually thought to involve the rebellion of Satan and his angels who were cast down to earth from heaven – God determined to destroy the earth. This was carried out through a great cataclysm which wiped out all animal species. The chaos of the second verse of Genesis is believed to indicate this event. This it does if one translates the word "was" by our English word "became." "And the earth *became* without form and void and darkness was upon the face of the deep." The surface of the earth was in a chaotic state through the destruction of that prior creation. After the cataclysm, God reconstructed the world with the creation of animal life and man, the *process of reconstruction* taking the six literal, sequential days of Genesis 1.

The great appeal of this position is that it allows Christians to accept the most obvious evidences for a great age of the universe with its fossil life, yet permits them to subscribe to a literal, six-day creation account. Most of its proponents insistently reject any suggestion of biological evolution.

Progressive Creationism

Progressive creationism is a name for another view designed to preserve faith in the Biblical creation account. In general it is the position that God created life on earth through a series of outright creative acts, although the acts were separated by greater or shorter spans of geologic time, not simply hours of time.

The Swiss-born Louis Agassiz, one of America's great naturalists, a geologist, paleontologist, zoologist, embryologist, professor at Harvard and a contemporary of Charles Darwin, advocated a progressive creation. Although a theist, he did not advocate it on religious grounds but because it seemed as if this is exactly what the geological record demands. As he looked at rock sequences, he noted that new forms of life appear suddenly without any evidence of intermediate ancestors. After some millions of years the forms abruptly disappear to be replaced by new and different forms. He believed these sudden breaks evidenced successive times in the history of the earth when God arranged for the annihilation of prior forms and miraculously interposed new species. He could not accept evolution as a viable alternative, simply because there was no evidence for it in the fossil record.

As did Agassiz, contemporary progressive creationists hold that there was not just one great creation of life, but several, or perhaps a great many. God at various periods in the history of the earth created fundamental types of organisms. From these fundamental types, through a limited process of evolution, there came into being a great diversity of forms. Evolution took place, but served only as a means of creating diversity within restricted limits.

It is difficult for any observer of nature to avoid biological evidence for the emergence of new species of organisms from preexisting species. Careful analyses of populations of a great number of different kinds of plants and animals have been made. These analyses, which include a study of the chromosomes and various other chemical constituents of the organisms, show evolution going on all about us. Three-quarters of a century ago creationists would argue, "If evolution is true, where is the evidence that it is taking place today?" No longer is this possible. Hence advocates of progressive creation admit to a degree of evolution, but aver it is not true evolution. It is "microevolution." True evolution, "macroevolution," which would change a species into something substantially different, does not take place. Microevolution might produce the 145 species of swans, ducks, and geese from one originally created duck species, but through evolution an ancestral reptile could never give rise to both a duck and a fox. Thus all the different forms of tortoises on the Galapagos Islands which so impressed Charles Darwin, a different form on each island, are the product of microevolution including, presumably, the tortoises in the same genus on islands in the Indian Ocean. Nevertheless, an ancestor to the tortoises was the object of a creative act.

Providential Creationism

Another distinct option is *providential creation*. According to this construction, creation did not occur in six literal days or in a number of creative leaps, but happened gradually through God's active and direct involvement with the world. All life may have emerged from a single ancestor. The time required is whatever time is discovered by science.

The first published expression of the concept was by the zoologist St. George Jackson Mivart who, writing as a Christian, termed it *providential evolution*. Mivart was a contemporary and friend of Charles Darwin.[9] Mivart began as an Anglican, but in 1843 converted to Roman Catholicism. Darwin broke with Mivart when Mivart insisted that natural selection was inadequate to account for evolution, and criticized Darwin for ignoring God in his scheme. Mivart was able to reconcile evolution with the Scriptures by treating the creation passages in Genesis as allegory.

It would not be incorrect to use "theistic evolution" for this category. Unfortunately, the term theistic evolution has been badly misused by many evangelical writers, writers who have only the vaguest and most confused concept of what theistic evolution amounts to. It is commonly mistaken for deistic evolution, for process theology, and for a view to be described below under the term macrotheistic creationism, none of which is remotely similar to true theistic evolution. Some creationist writers have so ridiculed "theistic evolution" that use of the term closes the door to further discussion.

Around the beginning of the twentieth century the doctrine had some powerful theological protagonists. The Baptist theologian Augustus H. Strong, Professor James Orr of the United Free Church College of Glasgow, and the eminent Benjamin B. Warfield of Princeton Theological Seminary, come readily to mind. All three were advocates of the full inspiration of the Bible, all three fundamentalists of their day. Their careful reasoning, whether right or wrong, was lost in the shrill voices of the evolution-creation debates of the 1920s, lost by those who never took the trouble to distinguish between authentic theistic evolution and some widely unrelated theological constructions.

According to providential creationists, God is the express agent of creation. As the Creator he directs both physical and biological processes to bring about his creative designs. The first form of life did not come into being accidentally but emerged because God providentially brought together the right molecules under circumstances of his design. The subsequent variations in the progeny of the first protocell, and the forces that selected one better adapted cell over another to produce a progression of living forms, were deliberately arranged by God's all-wise and all-powerful activity. God was not a remote superintendent, he was present and intimately involved in every atomic detail. Throughout the course of evolutionary history there occurred no slight genetic variation, no modification of the environment, no strike of a predator, no invasion of a parasite, no seemingly trivial event that God did not in his own way control. What we see today, according to providential creationists, is the handiwork of a God who was and is involved minute-by-minute in every circumstance.[10]

Providential creationism is not without its own set of problems. Those who cannot accept it as the Christian answer, can readily find a whole arsenal of objections, the most obvious that it includes the offensive notion of evolution. Nevertheless, it is a concept to be considered, a concept that cannot be shooed away by claiming it puts God out of the picture. Furthermore it does not necessarily contradict the teachings of creation passages in the Bible, something to be demonstrated in subsequent chapters.

Macrotheistic Creationism

Unable to find just the right English word for a group of similar concepts, I have coined a new one. *Macrotheistic* derives from the Greek *macran*, meaning "far away," and *theos*, the Greek word for God. It is a word standing for several more or less related views which make God directly responsible for the original act of creation and for establishing the laws by which the universe operates. God is disconnected, "far away," from any superintendence of the evolutionary steps that followed, or at best, he is left as a somewhat remote guide to the process. This concept is altogether different from providential creationism (authentic theistic evolution), which sees God actively involved in every least detail of the unfolding of creation. Macrotheistic creationism says that God generally expected what would happen after the creative act, but neither predetermined nor directed what took place.

Macrotheistic creationism was carefully expounded by the Church of England priest Dr. Arthur Peacocke, at one time a physical chemist working with biological macromolecules. He wrote, *"God is the ultimate ground and source of both law ('necessity') and 'chance'. On this view God acts to create in the world through what we call 'chance' operating within the created order, each stage of which constitutes the launching pad for the next."* Hence, he goes on to explain, the world's natural history is open-ended. God Himself was not sure where everything would lead, but *"God the Creator explores in creation."* In other words, *"God took a risk in creation"* (all italics his.)

The influential Roman Catholic theologian Hans Küng, formerly a professor of Catholic Theology at the University of Tübingen in Germany but censured by the Vatican and dismissed from that post, takes a similar point of view. He wrote that "the world and man, together with space and time, owe their existence to God alone and to no other cause." Furthermore, "man is the great goal of the process of creation and the center of the cosmos," and "God's creation itself implies his gracious turning to the world and man." Then he explains that the universe is orderly. It has a determined pattern, since God created the laws by which it operates.

Nevertheless, he explains, there is a large element of *chance* within the universe. The chance process of selection and evolution is an inescapable necessity. So creation comes into being through a process of growth as its gigantic system of laws interacts with wonderfully great and complex random events. He quotes approvingly from a 1976 work by R. Riedl, *The Strategy of Genesis. Natural History of the Real World* [in German] as follows:

> A *world* resulting from this strategy is neither a pure product of chance, nor is it planned in advance; man is neither meaningless, . . . nor was he aimed at . . . And the harmony of the world is neither a fiction nor is it prestabilized. Its harmony is poststabilized; it is a consequence of its growing systems.[11]

Undirected evolution brought everything into being but did so through God's involvement in setting up the principles for its operation.

Is macrotheistic creationism an anti-Biblical position? Its advocates range from those who uphold the inspiration of Scripture to those who are marginally theistic.[12] John Polkinghorne, a respected Church of England theologian and physicist, is clearly on the orthodox side of the ledger so far as his understanding of the person and work of Christ is concerned, even though he holds a truncated view of Biblical inspiration. With respect to creation, he wrote, "The apparently ambivalent tale of evolutionary advance and extinction . . .

is understood by the Christian as being the inescapably mixed consequence of a world allowed by its Creator to explore and realize, in its own way, its own inherent fruitfulness."[13] Yet he allows God some measure of "top-down" general control of things in the world. A large concern of his is to understand how God, who is not material in our ordinary understanding of nature, is able to exercise input into a material universe. He believes that "non-energetic" information is capable of providing a preferential direction to quantum events, and believes that God can provide such information. In his book, *Belief in God in an Age of Science*, 63-75, he shows how an understanding of physics allows for this possibility.

Howard J. Van Till is a thoroughgoing theist and a recognized evangelical with a high view of Biblical inspiration, yet his view, in my opinion, shares more with macrotheistic creationism than any other. Perhaps it should be placed in a category by itself. He believes that at creation God endowed matter with a "robust capacity" for self-organization and transformation, which provided for an unbroken line of evolutionary descent. God is responsible for the capability of life to evolve, but the process itself lacks his immediate direction. He terms his view "the fully gifted creation perspective;" gift referring to the capacity God bestowed on creation. In 1995 he wrote, "The formative history of the creation does not occur independently of God's action, but is continuously dependent on God's action of sustaining and blessing."[14] He did not clarify how God sustains and blesses within his model. His view is that God from the beginning established all the necessary laws, materials and interacting circumstances to bring each detail of creation into being.

Is macrotheistic creationism an odd bulge in the Christian tent, or completely outside? Certainly some of its modifications, such as that of Van Till, are within, and with some reservations, that of

Polkinghorne. According to most proponents, the steps of evolution are the result of interactions of random, undirected events. These events are limited only by natural laws. Unlike the naturalists, these creationists have a personal God who is responsible for the establishment and maintenance of the laws. Nevertheless, this concept seems to make God much less than the sovereign God of the Bible. Yet to condemn as an heretic or apostate an individual macrotheistic creationist who professes faith in the crucified and risen Savior would be to make a serious judgment beyond what is written.

Naturalistic Evolution

The prevailing non-Christian position needs to be considered, if only to clarify by contrast the preceding views. Most evolutionists today, lacking faith in a personal God, hold to *naturalistic evolution*. This is the concept that evolution happens because of accidental changes in gene structure, changes known as *mutations*. These changes may be useful or not. Ordinarily they are not. A randomly changing environment is also a requirement for evolution.

It is obvious to any observer that in some respects the environment is constantly changing, but there are also a thousand cryptic, little-observed changes. Without a change in the environment, a species persists unchanged. When the environment changes, a species simply dies out if its genetic traits are a handicap. The species survives if one or more mutations happen to produce an adaptation favorable to successful living in the changed environment. With the beneficial adaptation, the species both survives and gives rise to progeny possessing the change. In time, by the same process, its progeny may undergo further changes. Evolution is essentially a long succession of such changes.[15] The process goes by the name of *natural selection*, for it is the environment that selects those forms that carry the useful mutations. The mutations and the environmental changes are neither controlled by divine consciousness nor are they built into nature by a plan of God.

It should not be difficult to see why scientists (whether secular scientists or macrotheistic creationists) find this position so compelling. Much of science is founded on statistical probabilities. Gregor Mendel, the Austrian monk who first discovered the elementary principles of genetics, based his observations on statistical probabilities. Today the vast science of genetics is based on probabilities.[16] Where is God in determining whether a child will be born with Down's syndrome, with schizophrenia, with Huntington's syndrome, or with a defective gene producing muscular dystrophy?

A human geneticist who is counseling concerned parents, one of whom has a relative with a severe, disabling, genetic disease, can examine their family histories and report their chances of having a child with the trait. The geneticist can never say, "Yes, your next child will have the trait," or "No, your child will be free of the trait." All the geneticist can say is, "The mathematical probability is such and such." With sophisticated chemical analysis of the parents' blood and study of their DNA, the geneticist may be able to give a narrower range of probabilities, but he or she is still dealing with matters of chance.

Obviously evolution means something enormously different to an evolutionary naturalist and to a providential creationist, even if the outcomes seem identical. In the popular mind evolution is evolution. There is no point in wrestling over fuzzy distinctions. Man either came from an ape or he didn't. The difference, however, is important to naturalistic evolutionists. They most definitely do not want to be tethered with the theists. To them evolution has no goals and is directed by nothing but random forces. Evolution did not proceed toward some glorious endpoint, namely the production of mankind. It is nothing more than the constant adaptation of organisms to constantly changing environments. Richard Dawkins makes this point repeatedly in his books on the theory of natural selection, illustrated by the following famous quotation.

> Natural selection, the blind, unconscious, automatic process which Darwin discovered, and which we now know is the explanation for the existence and apparently purposeful form of all life, has no purpose in mind. It has no mind and no mind's eye. It does not plan for the future. It has no vision, no foresight, no sight at all. If it can be said to play the role of watchmaker in nature, it is the *blind* watchmaker.[17]

If life were to start all over again, it would be highly unlikely to produce humans or most of the species that we now recognize. It would go some independent way, depending on which mutations might occur out of the many thousands possible and what changes might occur in the environment.

It must be emphasized that the conclusion that nothing other than random, undirected forces are responsible for evolutionary change is not a conclusion of science itself. Scientists obviously observe no subtle forces directing evolution or, for that matter, any other physical process. Everything in nature appears to work on the same principle that governs which side comes up with the toss of a coin, and just about everyone agrees that this is pure chance. Absent any evidence of God in the process of evolution, most biologists feel constrained to believe that nothing but chance is in ultimate control. As the late evolutionary biologist Ernst Mayr explained,

> Darwinism rejects all supernatural phenomena and causations. The theory of evolution by natural selection explains the adaptedness and diversity of the world solely

materialistically. It no longer requires God as creator or designer.[18]

Nevertheless, this is a metaphysical belief, for the possibility of an underlying direction is at least conceivable, something that will be considered further along.

The Place to Start

For the person who believes the Bible, which of these views is acceptable? Is it possible there is a Biblical view which, on the whole, is in harmony with modern science? Or should a Christian treat scientific theories of the history of life with total skepticism, trusting solely on the plain language of God's inspired Word? The answer hangs on what is genuinely included in the plain language of God's inspired Word.

Do the Biblical creation accounts say what long tradition credits them with saying? If we take the first three chapters in the Bible in their historical and grammatical sense, what do they really say? Historical sense means the sense intended by the original authors and understood by the first readers.

Some Christians suppose certain Scriptures ought to bear a different meaning today than was intended by the author and understood by the first readers. Yet should this be true, all hope of a rational interpretation of the Bible is at an end. If the criterion for understanding the creation passages or any other Biblical passage is the personal response of the modern reader rather than what the author consciously intended, discussion itself is at an end. That is so, even if, as some believe, the Holy Spirit may direct a Christian to see a different meaning than the words actually convey.

The place to start is an examination of the creation passages. Can we get back to their original meaning? To be sure, there are points of uncertainty, but there are certain interpretations which seem impossible for the original authors to have had in mind. When we eliminate the more unlikely interpretations, we also may be removing impediments to contradictions with valid science. Before considering what may or may not be valid science, we need to consider the interpretation of the creation passages. After that, we can look at what science may have to say.

CHAPTER 2

THE SIGNIFICANT SILENCE OF GENESIS 1

Probably all evangelicals firmly believe that God is both author and agent of creation. Everything that a person sees is what God brought into being. This is their faith because it is the teaching of Scripture: "In the beginning God created the heavens and the earth." This statement in Genesis 1:1 could not be more explicit. It is reinforced by scores of statements throughout the Bible regarding the divine origin of the physical world, of life, of mankind.

What does the Bible say about the *time* when creation took place? Here the Christian needs to think through the actual words. Carefully scrutinizing each creation passage, it will be plain enough the Bible has *nothing* to say about the time of creation. What do the Scriptures say about the method God used in creation? Again, when a reader looks at the Scriptures objectively and attentively, they are found surprisingly silent. These issues simply are not addressed.

To a great many evangelical Christians, such thoughts border on the scandalous. A reading of the first chapter of Genesis seems to tell us plainly enough that God began and finished his creative work in six, successive, twenty-four hour days. The method, so far as God's methods can be investigated, involved six, spoken, divine commands. How could anyone presume to think that Genesis is silent regarding the time or method of creation?

In spite of the sense given by a casual reading of Genesis 1, the chapter refuses to provide us with answers to how and when. Some other perplexing questions are also left unanswered. Yet going beyond our English translations, the original language unveils answers to questions we never thought to ask. The chapter is full of surprises.

Before going further, an important caution is in order. Searching for the intended meaning of an ancient document, one written in a language quite different than ours and written by an author living in a different culture, certain principles of interpretation must be followed. A reader needs to be aware of language conventions that differ from our way of expressing thoughts. Some principles of particular importance will be noted as the study proceeds.

The Primary Function of Genesis 1

As a first principle, observe that *repetition for emphasis* is a device used with great regularity by authors of the Old Testament. This is a principle that has not been contested. It has been observed by orthodox and liberal scholars alike, but strangely enough has been ignored by many of those debating the meaning of Genesis 1. Whichever way the days of creation are to be interpreted, the principle of repetition declares that certain primary statements take center stage. Everything else is subordinate to four emphasized subjects: (1) God is the agent of creation, (2) creation is intrinsically good, (3) creation is orderly, and (4) mankind is created in the image of God.

1. God is the Agent of Creation.

Verse 1 states, "In the beginning God created the heavens and the earth." The remainder of the chapter is filled with assertions that God is the one who brought every facet of the world into being. Biblically, the fact of his creatorship of all that exists is indisputable.[19]

The truth of his creatorship is emphasized by repeated statements that he named what he made. In Hebrew thinking, a name is applied by someone who is sovereign to that which is named. A father names his child; an owner names a domestic animal; it was Pharaoh Neco who changed the name of Eliakim to Jehoiakim, his vassal king of

Judah; it was the king of Babylon who renamed Daniel as Belteshazzar; it was God who changed the name of Jacob to Israel. So in Genesis 1, God named the light "Day," he named the darkness "Night," he named the firmament "Heaven," he named the dry land "Earth," he named the waters the "Seas." He had the authority to do this because he created all of them.

It is hard to believe these assertions of God's creative activity were written other than as a response to a clear need. Without doubt, the Hebrews in the days of Moses and throughout the period of Judges were in constant danger of being seduced by Egyptian religious thinking.[20] A people cannot live four hundred years in a culture such as the Egyptian without being greatly influenced by it. Most likely the statements referring creation to one God were directed against Egyptian influences.[21] At the foundation of Egyptian religion was their cosmology – or perhaps we should say cosmologies, for there were numerous variations, although all somewhat related. Briefly scanning them allows us to see the importance of Genesis 1: 1.

In the Pyramid Texts, which came from Heliopolis about the middle of the third millennium B.C., there was alleged to have been a primordial abyss of water, without form or color, called Nun. Out of this shapeless material was born an early deity, Atum, who began the work of creation. At some later period Atum became identified with the sun god Re. Through an act of masturbation, Atum-Re begot two other gods, Shu and Tefnut. From these two were created the earth and the sky, male and female respectively. Through the centuries this initial religious thought was modified in various directions, but the foundation remained.

Against such a backdrop of religious confusion, Genesis reveals the all-powerful, all-wise, sovereign God, the only reasonable object of faith for his people. The Hebrew people needed to have a written statement of the infinitely great superiority of the true God. Reinforcing the statement of Genesis 1:1 is the repeated formula, beginning with verse 3, "Let there be. . ." This is a literary expression to say things came into being by the will of God. The literary formula "And it was so," says in effect there was no other will.

2. Creation Is Intrinsically Good.

A second emphatic point is that no part of God's creation in and of itself is evil, but all is good. This is stated in verse 4 and reiterated in verses 10, 12, 18, 25 and 31.

Christian writers have offered a number of explanations why Genesis 1 so repeatedly attributes goodness to creation. A common but almost silly explanation is that God was happy with each of his creative acts. Does not the six-fold repetition demand something more significant than that? Is God doing no more than clapping over his new artwork?

Considering the religious milieu of Egypt, there is a satisfactory and even necessary reason for emphasizing the goodness of creation. Egyptian religion thought of gods who created different aspects of the world. Some created benign things; others created evil parts of nature that bring suffering to mankind. Amon-Re was the king of the gods, but high on the pantheon of gods was the goddess Ma'at, who represented the deified concept of world order and who brought goodness, balance, harmony and truth into the world. Then there was the god Seth, who represented chaos, evil and confusion. Laid at the feet of Seth were storms, drought and other natural calamities, the evil aspects of the world. In stark contrast to a religion that found evil in matter or some aspects of matter, Genesis 1 proclaims in prophetic voice that God created a good world. The Hebrew scholar Gerhard von Rad observed that in verse 31 the formula approving the entire work of creation, "Behold, it was very good," can correctly be translated "completely perfect."[22] In and of itself, material substance is in no way evil. Insistence on this was necessary for God's people living under polytheistic influences.

3. Creation Is Orderly

Another major point designated by repetition is the orderliness of God's creation. All living things are made "according to their kinds." This is stated in verses 11, 12, 21, 24, and 25. In verses 11 and 12 and again in 29 there is the added emphasis of seeds specific to each kind of plant.

In the beginning of the evolution controversy, evangelicals understood the expression "after their kind" to teach that each biological species was designed to continue from generation to generation exactly as it was created. One species does not arise from another by evolution, for God made every species just as it is today. Most creationists today, whether believing in a young earth or an old earth, recognize that species do in fact change. So instead of using the word species, they take *kind* to mean some group consisting of one to several hundred or more biological species. The *kind* is a basic creative unit, a unit in which a range of variation might show up in the offspring, but a unit that does not evolve into creatures with quite different structures. Is this what Genesis 1 means when it uses the expression "after their kind?" What alternative interpretations are there? There are at least two others.

Some expositors understand the expression to mean simply, "every kind." The words then express the fact that all living things have come from God. Nothing arises by accident, by the command of some other god, or by spontaneous generation. Many of the ancients believed that toads were generated from mud, and flies were generated spontaneously from carrion. By using this translation, the NRSV gives the expression this meaning: "Then God said, 'Let the earth put forth vegetation: plants yielding seed, and fruit trees of every kind on earth that bear fruit with the seed in it.'" This is grammatically possible and, if true, would convey the thought that God's creation is all-extensive. There is no living thing for which God is not responsible.

Is this understanding acceptable? It is not necessarily wrong, and like certain treatments administered by physicians obeying the Hippocratic Oath, it does no harm and may be helpful.

Another possibility is that "after their kind" means that living organisms reproduce faithfully. Wheat seeds do not grow into barley plants. Horses do not occasionally produce asses. Ibis eggs never hatch into snakes. The Egyptians really were not convinced of this, although it must have followed from their everyday observations. They lived in a world governed, according to their religious system, by spells and irrational whims of their deities. The Hebrews needed to know they had a God who was altogether orderly in his creative work. He designed organisms with reproductive reliability.

This understanding most nearly fits the religious environment surrounding the people of Israel at the time Genesis was given through Moses. To suppose the words were written to deny the possibility of any change of the created *kinds* seems by far the least probable meaning. Why would Genesis address such a question? It would have been meaningless to those early Israelites. In their culture an obvious concern was whether the universe was governed by one sovereign God of order or a legion of the capricious and undependable gods of the Egyptians. It seems most unlikely they would have understood by *kind* some category much broader than the obvious species. They would not have thought of a lion *kind* that included the house cat, which the Egyptians had domesticated, nor would they have thought of the horse *kind* which would have included the ass. If to the early Hebrews *kind* meant a boundary beyond which change could not occur, they most naturally would have taken it to be the kinds with which they were familiar, those plants and animals that today we recognize as biological species.

It may be that nature was created without any evolution at all, not even the limited range of evolution allowed by young-earth creationists. But this series of affirmations about God creating things after their kind does not necessarily state or imply as much. If it states anything modern, it is that God is responsible for Mendelian genetics! God is the God of order and law!

4. Creation of Mankind is in The Image Of God

A fourth inescapable emphasis in Genesis 1 is that mankind is different from the animal world in essential nature. Obviously man has a body resembling that of animals in form and function. Man's brain, so far as has been observed, differs from that of other primates only in a much larger degree of development. But totally unlike the beasts of the field or any other creature, *man, male and female*, is created by God "in Our image, according to Our likeness." This is declared in verse 26 and repeated twice so that no one can miss its significance. Coupled with this statement is the command in verse 26 that mankind is to *rule* over all the other creatures, a command repeated for emphasis in verse 28.

Of what does the "image of God" consist? Whatever it means, it has been the subject of endless speculation and debate. Gordon J. Wenham discusses six views that have enjoyed support among Biblical scholars, then argues that the strongest case can be made that man is God's representative and his life is sacred.[23] But Wenham also notes that the language suggests that man is a copy of something that had

33

the divine image, not necessarily a copy of God himself. (The inversion of the meaning, that the passage is comparing God to man, demonstrating that God is a physical being with the appearance of a man, most certainly cannot be maintained!) Man is made "*in* the divine image" just as the tabernacle was made "*in* the pattern" shown Moses when he met with God on Mount Sinai. Perhaps Genesis is comparing man to the angels who worship in heaven. Both man and the angels have a similar function. Both praise God, either on earth or in heaven. Yet Wenham observes, "But even if angels bear the divine image, we are still left with isolating what it is that God, the angels, and men have in common that constitutes the divine image."

It must be that the early readers of Genesis knew what was intended by "the image of God," but with our present knowledge, what they understood remains obscure. Von Rad observes that the text speaks less of the nature of God's image than of its purpose.[24] Without knowing its precise nature, what is of cardinal importance in this chapter is abundantly clear. It is that *mankind is set apart*. Humans are not just measurably different from animals. Humans belong to a completely different order of being. Whether man's body was created by a direct fiat – direct command – of God or by a divinely directed process, by no means is man to be equated with animals. Mankind has a totally different worth. This is strongly implied in the command for man to exercise dominion over the animals.

Another question lacks a clear answer in Genesis 1: the answer to the question *how* (so important to us) is totally lacking. It is absent at this point because the question is outside the author's intent. Does the passage say that man was created in an instant of time, or does it allow man's creation to have been through a longer process? Perhaps the answer is given in the second chapter, but verses 26-30 are silent.

There are two ways verse 26 can be understood. The usual way is, "Let us make man and, in the process of doing so, let us make him in our image." It is as though we were to speak the word "man" more emphatically than other words in the sentence. What takes thought is man created instantaneously as a bipedal, beautifully structured, highly intelligent being, who *simultaneously* is made in the image of God. Support for this understanding comes from the thrice repeated use of the Hebrew word *bara'*, "create," in verse 27. This is the same word used in 1:1. Commenting on this verse, von Rad says that the word "contains the idea both of complete effortlessness and *creatio ex nihilo*, since it is never connected with any statement of the material."

On the other hand, if we were to read the passage out loud and emphasize the words "image of God," we would conjure a different picture. Paraphrased, the passage would read, "Let us now create man (whose body we have already made) in our image." This is grammatically allowable. It is different in that priority is assigned the *image*. The word *bara* in 1:27 can still have the sense assigned to it by von Rad of creation out of nothing, but apply not to the creation of man's physical body but the creation of man's immaterial and eternal spirit.

What are the implications of the second view? First, it more emphatically separates mankind from the animal world. Second, it does not require but definitely *allows* the body of man to have been formed by a directed process from a lower, non-human stock. Most evangelical creationists, whether accepting a young earth or an old earth, are united in complaining that any such interpretation ignores the plain meaning of this and the following verse. But the reader needs to back up a bit. This verse does not prohibit, it only *allows* the concept that man's body could have been the subject of a long creative process. What the verse clearly states is that man, at one specific point in time, was created as man in the image of God. So far as the verses are concerned, this could have been at the moment of the creation of man's physical body or sometime after.

With a long tradition of reading verses 26-27 in a particular way, it may be difficult to accept, but if examined fairly, the verses do not of themselves lend unequivocal support to any of the options advocated by the various schools of creationists. The plain intent of the verses is to emphasize the unique status of mankind in creation, an emphasis appropriate not only to the purposes of Genesis 1 but to the entire Bible.

These are the four primary emphases of Genesis 1. Only after realizing that these are the real issues are we ready to consider the meaning of the seven days. The interpretation of the days is where such great controversy has centered, although inappropriately. The days carry a secondary, not a primary emphasis. Expositors have generally focused on secondary rather than primary issues.

The days of Genesis 1

Is the description of the days the language of poetry? Poets are given license to emphasize a message by employing extravagant figures. No, the words are not poetic. The structure of the lines does not exhibit the parallelism characteristic of Hebrew poetry. The words are highly stylized but nonetheless narrative in form.[25] But even if they are poetic figures of speech, what message would they be intending to convey? The extravagant language of a poet is still directed toward a meaning.

A possible solution was expressed by Wenham, who said that, "at best, all language about God is analogical."[26] When we try to describe God and his acts, we are limited to words that make sense when describing human deeds. But the person and work of God are on such an unimaginably different plane the task is impossible. The best any human language can do, even when inspired by the Holy Spirit himself, is to picture a resemblance. In a picturesque way the six days, without seeking to convey specific information, stand for God's incredibly complex and indescribable activity in creation. This removes from the interpretation any need to ask when or how creation took place, and how to explain the multifarious fossils in our paleontological museums.

It might afford the Christian a measure of relief to follow Wenham here. If we do, someone might ask what principle of interpretation tells us when and if a passage is to be taken analogically and when it is straightforward. It may be that Wenham's solution is correct, but it does not follow from any very clear and theologically consistent principle of interpretation.

If in contrast, the days are to be taken in some direct sense, what sense is it? The following are major proposed interpretations of the days under the following headings: literal, 24-hour, successive days, each day representing an age of time, days of a reordering of creation following an original creation and judgment of that creation, literal days describing a local span of creative work, the days a panorama of a great span of time, days on which God related what he had done in creation, and days representing themes or categories of creation. Within most of these views are variants of greater or lesser scope. The list is not exhaustive, but probably includes any proposed idea that deserves serious consideration.

1. Literal 24-Hour, Successive Days
Whether we, who want to discover concordance between science and the normal sense of Scripture, find it to our liking, a great many competent Biblical commentators are satisfied that the days are

intended to be understood as actual, 24-hour, successive days. Should we agree, different possibilities seems to follow.

For one, we can simply admit there is no expectation of reconciling science and Scripture. If we opt for the Christian faith, we simply place science and religion into separate compartments. Why try to reconcile them when there is no existential or spiritual need to do so?

Some may be satisfied with such a schizophrenic division, but for most people the Scriptures may as well be discarded if they are open to factual question. Surely God is as capable of revealing truth concerning the material world he created as he is of providing teaching concerning himself and his purposes.

A possibility chosen by a large number of present-day evangelicals, is to take the words for what they appear to say and bend science to fit. If some recalcitrant conclusions of science cannot be accommodated, then the conclusions must be put down as bad science. Nevertheless, those who choose this path have to do some serious bending themselves. Light and darkness (day and night) start on the first day. The sun is not created until the fourth day. Henry M. Morris in *The Genesis Record* gets around the problem of days and nights before creation of the sun by postulating that God brought into being a source of light "corresponding to the sun" to produce the first three days and nights.[27] Seriously? It would have to have been a remarkably strong light source, at least a source in the magnitude of the sun to illuminate the whole earth. What object produced this light? What happened to the object? Dr. Morris does not say. The notion is an example of making up an improbable explanation to support a preconceived interpretation.

On the other hand, E. H. Andrews of the University of London proposed that on each of the creative days God simply suspended or replaced natural laws for a moment of time to achieve his creative purposes.[28] Andrews did not specify which laws were suspended but left the problem to the omnipotence of God. He found alternative views unacceptable, particularly "theistic evolution," which, unfortunately, he misunderstood.

Is it possible that we simply cannot honestly read the chapter in its normal, literary sense without consenting to the young-earth understanding of literal, 24-hour, successive days? In seeking any other sense are we simply trying to escape what is uncomfortable and difficult? In weighing the question, one cannot overlook the force of Exodus 20:11:

> For in six days the LORD made the heavens and the earth, the
> sea and all that is in them, and rested the seventh day;
> therefore the LORD blessed the sabbath day and made it holy.

One can hardly consider this figurative language. It is an integral part of the Fourth Commandment. It is part of the cultural context as well as the more remote literary context of Genesis 1. If this passage says that God created the world in six days, then it would seem all argument is at an end. This may well be the strongest evidence for understanding the days as successive, literal days. Unsurprisingly, the young earth *Creation Research Society Quarterly* has this verse on its masthead stating its avowed faith.

With this, are we not also obliged to consider Exodus 31:17? Considered carefully, this verse throws a glitch into the argument. Here God speaks through Moses and says that on the seventh day God "ceased *from labor*, and was refreshed." To say that God was "refreshed" intimates that the days might not be as literal as first appears. We can be sure our omnipotent God does not need to be refreshed. In these words we have what grammarians term an anthropomorphism. It is a figure of speech in which, for the sake of emphasizing a point, human feelings are attributed to God. Exodus 31:17 suggests that in Exodus 20:11 the references to the days is not a commentary upon Genesis 1, but is a pattern or a model for the command regarding observance of the Sabbath.

If we demand seven, successive, 24-hour days, we are left with a less than satisfactory interpretation. Although accepted by the great majority of evangelicals, it raises problems that throw doubt on the validity of Scripture.

2. The Day-Age Hypothesis

Historically many believing scientists found it possible to harmonize Scripture with geology by taking each day of Genesis to represent a vast age of time. This included two pioneering American geologists, J. W. Dawson and James Dana, the great American botanist Asa Gray, and many others. Interestingly, scientists who are Christians have been the chief proponents of the view, not the commentators. In recent years the hypothesis has been vigorously defended by the geologist Davis A. Young[29] and by the astronomer and Christian apologist Hugh Ross.[30] The interpretation is useful in that it allows a Christian or an orthodox Jew to preserve a view of the authenticity of Scripture while holding to a great age for the earth. The concept begins with the observation that Psalm 90:4 and 2 Peter 3:8 speak of one day in the sight of God being as a thousand years.

Added to this, one can find general concordance between the scientific history of the universe and the events described for each day. The concordance seems to provide convincing support for the day-age concept. If each day corresponds to the events in time discovered by science, what better proof is needed? Ross lists the creation events as follows. There was the initial creative act bringing space, time, matter, energy, galaxies, stars, planets, etc., into being. Day 1 was the transformation of the earth's atmosphere from opaque to translucent. Day 2 was the formation of a stable water cycle, a lengthy process. Day 3 was the establishment of continent(s) and ocean(s) and production of plants on the continents. Day 4 was transformation of the atmosphere from translucent to transparent (Sun, Moon and stars become visible for the first time, having been occluded in all previous ages). On day 5 God brought into being small sea animals and sea mammals, a long period before the events of day 6. Day 6 was the making of land mammals and the creation of mankind.

In order to evaluate this view, a short excursus on an important principle of Biblical interpretation will be helpful. This is the principle of adhering to the *historical/cultural* meaning of a passage. Unless we understand the Scriptures in the sense intended by the original authors, and as they were understood by the first readers, any consistent interpretation would seem forever out of reach. In lieu of an historical understanding, what valid rule might one imagine to arrive at a consistent and reliable interpretation? If the meaning is different for our age than it was for people three thousand years ago, who or what is to determine its meaning? Language, in order to communicate, depends on words understood by both the writer and the reader in a context of associated words and ideas, all of which are part of a commonly experienced or understood culture. Word meaning, historical context, and cultural conventions are interdependent. Being intertwined, all three must somehow be considered together to get the meaning intended by the writer. In our ordinary speaking and writing we do this unconsciously. But when we are reading something written by an author from another culture and another age, we need to take pains to think about each expression. Not to do so may be to miss the author's real meaning, or to read into a passage something never intended. When considering creation passages, these elements are most important if we would know what God is saying to us.

The day-age view falters on this very point. It is quite improbable that the Hebrews would have understood the days as vast periods of time. There seems to be no historical circumstance or cultural reason for this interpretation. Although Psalm 90:4 speaks of a thousand years in the sight of God being like a day that has just gone by, it is most unlikely that the author was seeking to establish a time definition of *day*.

The day-age theory runs into another great difficulty. If the ages are sequential (day-age one, day-age two, etc.), a number of embarrassing problems result. How could there be plants in existence an age before the animal creatures, which include not only the "great sea monsters" but also "every living creature that moves"? Plants are dependent upon carbon dioxide produced by the animal world, just as animals are dependent upon plants to produce oxygen. Another difficulty is that aquatic and flying creatures are brought forth on the fifth day, whereas terrestrial animals do not appear until the sixth day. True, very primitive "plants" (blue-green bacteria) come first in the geological record, and aquatic animals come before terrestrial animals. But birds appear long after the first terrestrial animals.

Could it be that each day is an age, but the ages are broadly overlapping? Yes, but that would make the words "evening and morning" meaningless. "Evening and morning" do not need to be taken as specifying 24-hour days. They may simply be figures of speech for "beginning and ending." But if so, and if the ages are broadly overlapping, the words would seem to be without significance. We can hardly believe that the repeated phrase "evening and morning" lacks meaning.

3. The Ruin and Reconstruction Theory

A view expounded in 1804 by the Scottish Presbyterian clergyman Thomas Chalmers takes the first verse of Genesis to speak of an original creation in the dateless past. This creation populated the earth with the legion of now extinct species described by the paleontologists. The view allows for the span of time found by the geologists. For some reason God's wrath brought destruction upon that earlier creation. The second verse describes the resulting chaos on earth. The consequence of the judgment was that the earth *became* "without form and void." The rest of the chapter then describes God's work in *reconstructing* the earth as an habitation for mankind. The view, as previously mentioned, was popularized in evangelical circles by Pember's book *Earth's Earliest Ages*, first printed in 1876 and frequently republished.[31] Later, the *Scofield Reference Bible* brought it to the attention of the Christian public. Because, according to this view, there is a space of time between the first and second verses, it is often dubbed the "gap theory."

Advocates make a distinction between the word *bara'* translated "create" in 1:1, 1:21 and 1:27 and the word *asah*, usually translated "make." *Bara'* is to make something entirely new or novel. In the Old Testament the word is only used of God's creative work, not of man's. On the other hand *asah* means to "make something functional." Hence there is no problem with God bringing about the events of days one through three, yet not making the sun until day four. The sun was created along with the earth and the rest of the universe at the beginning. The judgment left the earth in some kind of disorganized swamp covered by the densest fog. The first day the fog was dissipated sufficiently that light from the sun penetrated to the earth's surface bringing distinct daylight. The second day the fog lifted so that there was an expanse of clear air between the surface and the clouds above.

The clouds were still so dense, however, that the sun itself was not visible.

The third day the waters began to drain from the ground, and as the dry land appeared the ground brought forth vegetation. It is not said that plants were *created* on the third day. Where did they come from? From spores and seeds left from the earlier creation. On the fourth day the sun and the moon were made, that is they were made functional, made visible. The fifth day the waters "swarmed" with all the creatures that move in the waters. They were not created on the fifth day, but were survivors of the judgment. On the fifth day they proliferate. Winged creatures seem to have survived the cataclysm, but great sea monsters (whales?) were created brand new. On the sixth day it is not clear that all vertebrate animals were created new, but at least man was made from scratch.

Although at one time very popular with evangelicals, the theory has few current advocates. The scholarly Canadian, the late Arthur C. Custance, wrote a long defense of the view in 1970.[32] Proponents generally take the word "was" in verse 2 in the sense of "became," making the verse read, "And the earth became without form and void." Most Hebrew scholars consider this an inappropriate translation, although the NIV footnotes the word *was* with the comment: "Or possibly *became*." Nevertheless, the view does not absolutely depend on whether the word is translated *was* or *became*. Verse 2 may simply describe the state of the earth after the judgment.

Problems with the view are numerous. An analysis of the fossil record shows that throughout history a long and changing sequence of animals and plants occupied the world, not a single pre-Adamic creation. It also reveals several great cataclysms that destroyed a large percentage of forms then living, yet no cataclysm shortly before the appearance of mankind. Anyone seriously interested in the question might consult Waltke's *Creation and Chaos*, with its devastating analysis of the Hebrew grammar used to justify the theory.

4. The Local Creation Theory

This theory views the six creative days as work done by God in a limited region of the earth to make it suitable for the habitation of mankind. Since the Hebrew word for *earth* can legitimately be understood in the sense of *land*, some have considered all of Genesis 1 after the first verse to apply only to a divine work of rehabilitating a small portion of the earth. The viewpoint of the chapter's author is not what God did for the universe as a whole, not even for the globe in its entirety, but only for the span of geography essentially known to the author.

If this is a true interpretation, it affords considerable relief to the Christian seeking to reconcile science with Scripture. The chapter has nothing to do with geological ages, since the creation of the earth itself, described in verse 1, took place in earlier times by unspecified methods. The "creation" of the sun, moon, and stars on day four is no problem. The expression in verse 16, "And God made the two great lights," can well be understood of God making the sun, moon, and stars *appear* after having been obscured. The local setting eliminates the difficulty of trying to imagine a tremendously thick vapor cloud enveloping the whole earth. It would require no more than dense clouds over one part of the earth obscuring the source of the light. The command in verse 20 for the waters to "bring forth swarms of living creatures" is only a command for preexisting marine life suddenly to flourish in oceans where their growth for some unspecified reason had been inhibited. The creation in verse 21 of "great sea monsters" need not have taken place on day five, since the verb *create* is in a Hebrew tense saying no more than at a particular point they were created by God.

Continuing through the chapter to the creation of mankind, proponents could argue either of two ways. 1. Man as a physical being could have been created on the sixth day, or 2. man, whose body would have come from pre-human ancestors, could have been created in the image of God on the sixth day. If one takes the latter point of view, there would be no difficulty in other human-like beings living contemporaneously with Adam. These would be people in human bodies but lacking the "image of God." It could be one of these that Cain chose for his wife.

Did the author of Genesis 1 unwittingly describe the creative activity of God with respect to no more than a small section of the earth? Possibly, without being consciously aware that he was writing only of his own area. The Hebrew scholar John Sailhamer argued rather convincingly that after verse 1 the chapter deliberately takes a local view.[33] This is because the whole focus of Genesis is on God's purposes for Israel and his covenants with the nation.

The view, for all its advantages in solving the Bible/science conflict, has its own unsolved problems. Admittedly, the Old Testament and the Book of Genesis in particular may be mostly limited to God's dealings with Israel. That does not mean the first chapter has only Israel in view. The impression gained from a natural reading of the chapter is that a far more general theological statement is intended. Then too, we must ask if there is an interpretation that better fits the literary style of Genesis 1, and that magnifies the glorious power and wisdom of God, as a fitting prelude to the Book of Genesis, and, indeed, to the rest of the Bible. Possibly one is to be found in the thematic theory, the seventh in this list.

5. The Panorama Theory

I invite you to my home to view slides of my trip from New York to San Francisco. Out of politeness you accept but groan inwardly, expecting to view a daily travelogue of pictures. All I show you, however, are six slides, one each of Brooklyn Bridge, Lincoln's birthplace, Mt. Rushmore, Old Faithful Geyser, the Mormon Temple, and Golden Gate Bridge. "There," I exclaim, "you've seen my trip across the United States." You have indeed seen it, in the sense that you have witnessed a sampling of my trip. Is it not reasonable to believe that in some similar way Genesis 1 describes six days' work completed by God, but that the days are *not contiguous*? Gaps of indeterminate length may separate each of the days. Reading the chapter gives the impression that the days follow one after the other. Nevertheless, interpreting them as sample pictures of one long panorama is not forbidden, and has the great advantage of permitting the time span for creation required by astronomy and geology. It seems quite unlikely the ancients understood the days as separated by periods of time. Even so, could not the prescient Holy Spirit, who inspired the record, have given us an account that could be interpreted in the sense of days separated by great gaps? It would relieve us of a great deal of agony in squaring Genesis with the long aeons demanded by the geologists.

As satisfying as this explanation might seem, it runs into some of the same difficulties as other interpretations that try to stretch six days into a few billion years. The sun and the moon are not created until the fourth day, but plants, which are totally dependent on sunlight, on the third day. It could be that the sun was created in the beginning but was hidden by dense clouds until the fourth day. That does not, however, seem to be the thinking of the author. Verse 17 says God set the sun, moon, and stars in the firmament of the heavens to *give light upon the earth.* One might respond, "Yes, that refers to their *function*, but the fourth day only relates to their appearance." Nevertheless, it strains normal reading of the text to divide appearance from creation and function. The account also has the difficulty of postponing to the sixth day the appearance of "everything that creeps upon the ground," whereas plants appear on the third day. According to the geological record, although mammals did not appear until long after the first plants, millipedes and scorpions appear in the Silurian. This is simultaneous with the first vascular plants.

There are, to be sure, some interesting variations on the panorama interpretation. In one way or another, these variations attempt to get around the difficulties. Frederick H. Capron, a British scientist and Biblical apologist, noted in 1902 that the account of each day begins with a command.[34] This is followed by a statement that the command was carried out. He proposed that the command was made at a specific point, that is, on one particular day. The statement, which comes after the command, represents an account of the age-long process that followed. Thus in 1:3 God commanded "Let there be light." This was followed by a process that with our present knowledge we would think of as the formation of our planetary system from a primeval nebula. In due course this would be followed by the gravitational accumulation of particles to form a planetary mass. This mass would become a spinning world with days and nights. The same pattern obtains for day two and each successive day. There is a command separated by a shorter or longer period of time from the day that precedes it, followed by a long period of unfolding of the divine command. The age-long periods can be thought of as broadly overlapping each other. R. C. Newman and Herman J. Ecklemann, Jr., recently developed and expanded Capron's concept.[35]

Other variations of the panorama theory (each with an appropriate name donated by its author) have been proposed. The major difficulty with each variation of the panorama theory is the same problem found with the day-age hypothesis. It seems altogether unlikely that age-long periods would have been understood by the earliest readers of Genesis. If the author had intended each day to be a long age, the beginning of a long age, or the culmination of a long age, the language would have been much more specific than it is.

Perhaps we can reason that God in his wisdom presented an account that the Hebrews in their naivety would have interpreted one way, but that we moderns are capable of reading and ought to read in a different way. But for reasons I have suggested above, divine revelation does not work that way. The *meaning* of a passage of Scripture ought to be no different for us than it was for those who first received it. The major reason for so many conflicting views of the creation chapters is that people try to interpret them from a modern, not from the original perspective. Unquestionably, for modern mankind there are worshipful attitudes and moral *applications* flowing from creation passages, but the meaning belongs to the ancients.

6. The Revelation Theory

An ingenious reconciliation of Genesis 1 and science is P. J. Wiseman's concept that each day is a day in which God explained to Adam what he did in creation.[36] According to Wiseman, instead of reading, "God made the expanse," (or "firmament") we can legitimately read, "And God *showed* the firmament." The word for make (*asah*) should be understood in Genesis 1 as "show." In some forty-three Old Testament passages *asah* is translated "show" (e.g., Genesis 19:19). This view considers the days brief summaries of successive 24-hour days in which God related to Adam his work of creation. Hence the days are six *show-days*, six visions, six panoramas. At the end of the six days, God *rested* not from his work in general but from the specific work of narrating the story. Genesis 2:3 says that "God finished his work which he had done, and he rested on the seventh day."

The utility of this interpretation is that it removes the time element from the first chapter and allows a succession of geological periods (although Wiseman thought that all species were created right from the first, including man). There is no need to be concerned about the length of time God took in creation or the process he may have used, since Genesis 1 only catalogues the total span of God's creative work. The creation of the sun and moon, recounted on day 4, may have come after or it may have come before the creation of plants recounted on day 3. The difficulties of sequence are removed. The theory also explains how information about creation came into man's knowledge. If Adam was the endpoint of creation, he could not have personally observed what God did. It is only reasonable to think that God must have related it to him, either in some audible form or through realistic visions.

One difficulty with this interpretation is that the first chapter becomes a footnote to creation rather than an introductory declaration of God's power and majesty. Furthermore, on the surface, at least, the record does not profess to be a vision. Another major problem is that wherever else *asah* is translated "show," it is always in the sense of showing something to be so, exhibiting something, such as showing kindness or showing love. It has no attending idea of something visionary or pictorial. Wiseman was aware of this, but took the word back to a root meaning. Other Hebrew scholars, however, have not been convinced.

7. A Thematic Interpretation

An interpretation which sees each day as a majestic theme of God's creative acts avoids most of the problems attached to other interpretations. Such is the thematic interpretation, which treats each day as a category of creation. It is not a recent interpretation, although it has been overlooked (or perhaps ignored) by most creationist writers. Henri Blocher, who so ably expounded it, terms it "the literary interpretation" and traces it back to St. Augustine in the fifth century and Gersonides in the fourteenth century.[37] A century ago the Baptist theologian A. H. Strong adopted this interpretation, calling it the pictorial-summary interpretation.[38] The view has also been termed the "historico-artistic interpretation" and the "framework theory." The latter is possibly the most commonly used designation, but the name may imply some things that are not there.[39]

What is the evidence that in the mind of the human author (and so understood by the earliest readers) there was not a sequence of literal days but series of metaphorical days? Four strong pointers follow.

(a) Most remarkable is the narrative structure of Genesis 1:1-2:3 based on a stylized system of numerical harmony. Little of this can be gathered from reading an English translation, but it is there in the Hebrew. After the introductory verse, the section is divided into *seven* paragraphs. The paragraph divisions are marked by the recurring sentence, "And there was evening and there was morning, an *Nth* day." Each of the three nouns that occur in the first verse, *God*, *heavens*, and *earth*, express the basic concepts of the whole section. These are repeated in the section a certain number of times, but always in multiples of *seven*. *God* occurs five times seven (thirty-five times). *Earth* is repeated for a total of three times seven (twenty-one times). *Heavens* also is found three times seven (twenty-one times). The expression *it was good* appears *seven* times, the seventh time *very good*.

With respect to verses within the paragraphs, verse 1 has *seven* words and verse 2 *fourteen* words (2 x 7). *Water* is mentioned *seven* times in the course of paragraphs two and three. In the *seventh* paragraph describing the *seventh* day, there are three consecutive sentences, each of which consists of *seven* words and contains in the middle the expression *the seventh day*. The total number of words in the seventh paragraph total *thirty-five* (5 x 7).

What careful thought and planning must have gone into the construction of the chapter. Or could the Holy Spirit have so inspired it without the conscious knowledge of the human author? The latter is unlikely, but whichever the case, the craftsmanship shows that we have here no ordinary narrative. It is not a simple recitation of events. Something more is intended. This is further demonstrated by the way the paragraphs form a pattern.

(b) The structure of the paragraphs after the introductory sentence strongly suggests that no ordinary sequence of days is intended. The paragraphs correspond in a way that forms what E. W. Bullinger termed an extended alternation.[40] This is a common Hebrew literary device, often exhibited in the Psalms. The first topic corresponds with the fourth, the second with the fifth, and the third with the sixth. It can be represented as follows:

Day 1   Light

  Day 2   Sea and heaven

    Day 3   Earth with its plants

Day 4   Luminaries

  Day 5   Fish and that which flies in the heavens

    Day 6   Animals and man with plants for food

The third and sixth days are further highlighted by each having a double announcement of the divine word *and God said* and the approval formula *and God saw that it was good*. Hence they correspond formally.

Day seven corresponds with the first verse, since the terms *heaven and earth, God, create* reappear in reverse order to that of 1:1. On pages 6-7 of his commentary, Wenham calls this "an inverted echo of the opening verse." It serves to emphasize the distinctive importance of the seventh day.

Day 4 is in the middle of the week and is described at much greater length than anything except the creation of mankind. The full description of Day 4 indicates that the creation of the heavenly bodies held a special significance for the author. This being so, the position of each day depends not on when they occurred in time but on *significance*. That the structure focuses on the fourth day is not surprising in view of the deification of the sun and moon in Egyptian religion and in other ancient cosmologies. Genesis 1:14-18 declares that the luminaries are created objects, not creating gods. Accordingly their role is reduced to the function of lighting the earth and ruling the night and day as surrogates of God.

The description of the fourth day partakes of another literary device, which most modern literary critics term a *chiastic* structure. The name comes from its resemblance to the left half of the X-shaped Greek letter chi. The chiasma serves to direct our attention to the importance of the fourth day. It can be exhibited as follows:

A₁. To separate the day from the night (14a)

   B₁. for signs, and for seasons, and for days and years (14b)

      C₁. to give light on earth (15)

         D₁. to govern the day (16a)

         D₂. to govern the night (16b)

      C₂. to give light on the earth (17)

   B₂. to govern the day and the night (18a)

A₂. to separate the light from the darkness (18b)

What are we to make of this elaborate structure? What has it to do with our interpretation of the meaning of the days? If anything, the structure suggests that the human author's interest did not lie with the order of creative events but with the *effect* of creation.

(c) It is especially critical to note that the term "day" does not mandate a 24-hour period. The word *day* can be taken in the sense of "in the time that" or "at that time," or a "period of time." In its most common usage the word refers either to the time from dawn to sunset or to the 24 hours from sunset to sunset. In a number of places the context of the word shows that a secondary meaning is "time" or "period." So in Genesis 2:4 we read, "In the day that the Lord God made the earth and the heavens" Following this introductory clause is a description of the whole span of creation. Day in 2:4 refers to the *time* of creation. In a number of Old Testament passages the "day of the LORD" refers to a period of divine judgment, oftentimes seen to refer to a number of events extending beyond a single 24-hour day (for example, Isaiah 13:6; Joel 2:1 ff.; Zechariah 14:1-15). There is no reason *day* in the first chapter cannot have the same sense.

Those who dispute the interpretation cite the numbering of the days as evidence that a sequence of time was intended. The Hebrew scholar Cassuto pointed out, however, that when a group of objects exist at the same time and are considered together, the reader is able, momentarily, to pay attention to only one at a time.[41] For the reader's benefit, the author designates the first *one*. That being considered, the next is designated *two*, and so on. The NASB reflects this understanding by translating "one day," "a second day," "a third day," and so on, instead of "the first day," "the second day," "the third day," and so on.

(d) A convincing argument for the thematic view is found in the centrality of the fourth day. The author obviously exercised remarkable care in the composition of the chapter. We cannot believe the author was too stupid to notice there could not be day and night on the first, second, and third days without the presence of the sun, especially after he indicated in verse 17 the purpose of the two great lights. They are "to give light on the earth." Nor would Jewish readers have failed to notice this. There is evidence that under the direction of the Holy Spirit the Old Testament went through some degree of editing. The human editors would have noticed this glaring breech of consistency and would have emended it – had they not understood that themes or topics rather than a sequence of time was intended!

These four observations lead to a possible and most convincing interpretation. The days of Genesis 1 are themes or categories of creation. The notion of a specific time, whether long or short, is simply not there. The concept of sequence is not necessarily there. Even though the days are numbered, the reader's primary interest is directed to what was accomplished by the power of God. The creative items may have been overlapping, may have been separated by time, may have been simultaneous – the element of time is of no importance, but the topics are.

Perhaps the most telling argument against a thematic interpretation is the specification of evening and morning. "Evening and morning" as a single expression is not used in a clear sense of beginning and ending elsewhere in the Old Testament. Nevertheless, evening coupled with morning in Psalm 90:5-6 has the thought of a period much longer than a single day. Here the Psalmist compares mankind to grass in the field. "In the morning it flourishes and sprouts anew; Toward evening it fades and withers away." Surely the Psalmist did not intend his readers to think that grass sprouts in the morning and dies that very evening! But this is the way life seems to be. It is brief. Cannot the two words in Genesis 1 have a similar metaphorical use?

Those who want to think that the days are sequential, 24-hour days can take comfort in the conclusion of the redoubtable authorities C. F. Keil and F. Delitzsch, who consider "evening and morning" to define literal, 24-hour days.[42] They deny there is a genuine structure of correspondence in the passage, and hence reject a thematic interpretation. They also note the inclusion of the creation of man and animals on the sixth day. If categories of creation were intended, man as the significant apex of creation, they think, would surely have been treated in a separate category from the animals.

Robert A. Pyne, professor at Dallas Theological Seminary, questioned the view by observing there are no other evidences that this type of genre was known in Semitic literature, so it is unknown whether the ancient Hebrews would have recognized it as specifying themes of creation.[43] Interestingly, the study of literary structures of the Old Testament is a newly blossoming field. David A. Dorsey commented, "The field of research is still in its infancy."[44] Nevertheless, Dorsey described numerous examples of shorter and longer passages exhibiting similar corresponding structures. Apparently the Semitic mind, quite unlike our Western way of thinking, was attuned to this kind of presentation.

In spite of some thoughtful objections, the thematic concept, a concept emphasizing the doctrine of the incredible power and wisdom of God rather than specific times, brings the days into a meaningful focus within the chapter. The author seeks to picture what God performed, and to place it in a framework of days (hence the term "framework theory") to bring it within some grasp of the human mind, although what God accomplished no one, not even the most erudite twenty-first century cosmologist, can begin to fathom.

Even though there may be a margin of uncertainty about the choice of one of the seven options above, staunch young-earth creationists should observe that the view of an initial creation in six literal days is less well supported than any of the other interpretations. If a person accepts Wenham's proposal that the days are literal but analogical, he or she might reasonably interpret them as sequential periods of 24 hours each, but this would be meaningless for determining what the passage has to say about the age of the earth and the time of creation. On the other hand, the explanation of the days as themes of God's creative work leaves the interpreter with the closest conformity to the strategy of the passage itself, and the most satisfactory resolution of the difficulties. It solves such problems as the time when the sun was created in relation to other creative acts of God. It takes the issue of the age of the earth out of the picture altogether. If this view is true, there is no problem in reconciling geological time sequences with Genesis 1, for there is nothing to reconcile. Genesis 1 directs us to the power and supremacy of the Creator, and to the completion of his work in mankind, not to time and method.

Whether we are convinced the earth is young or believe the earth is old, we can rest easy with a thematic interpretation of the days of the first chapter. Chapters 2 and 3, which we consider next, are far more puzzling.

CHAPTER 3

GENESIS 2:4-3:24, A SURPRISING GENRE

For the person wondering what the Bible has to say about creation, the second account of creation in Genesis 2:4-3:24 seems to leave few doubts. Do not the words require a young earth? Rock strata that geologists consider very old often clearly show a pattern formed by raindrops in the now-solidified muds. According to 2:5 it had not rained on the earth prior to the time of the creation of man, and his fall into sin. Hence the "ancient" muds must have been formed *after* the fall, and it must be that "three hundred million year old strata" with raindrop impressions are no older than mankind. Who is right? The geologists, or our God-inspired Bible?

How does one bring science and these two chapters of Genesis into any semblance of harmony? On the surface the problems are much more intractable than those found in the first chapter. The section can be read in its most literal sense and, if taken this way, strongly supports the concept of a young earth. It would seem that any interpretation other than a literal one questions the authenticity and integrity of the Bible.

The Purpose of the Account

However one chooses to read it, whether in a literal sense or in some other sense, the primary purpose of the account is obvious. God brought the first humans into an ideal environment. Nothing better could be desired. The single prohibition God placed before Adam and Eve posed not the least excuse for disobedience. It was a simple prohibition that allowed them a choice without in any manner driving them to it. Yet Adam and Eve consciously disobeyed. The act separated them from fellowship with God and consigned them to a life of toil and death. At the same time they were given a promise of ultimate victory for their posterity.

The story is told with childlike simplicity. Yet it carries in its words the deepest spiritual insights. The ideal of marriage is reflected in the search for a perfect wife for Adam. The value of the wife is told by the search for a companion among all creatures, but none being found, she was created especially for his helpmate. Hence the husband should treasure her as much as himself. Significantly, she was made from his side. Cassuto commented: "Just as the rib is found at the side of the man and is attached to him, even so the good wife, the *rib* of her husband, stands at his side to be his helper-counterpart, and her soul is bound up with his."[45] When it is said, "They become one flesh," far more is intended than the significance of sexual union. Blood relations are one's "flesh and bone." Marriage is just as close a relationship and cannot prosper without each committing to the other as fully as each one is committed to father and mother, brother and sister.

The account of the temptation is uncomfortably characteristic of the inner debate that goes on in our own hearts as we give in to self-will, and seek to justify our actions. Addressing the woman, the serpent asks ingenuously, "Did God really say, 'You must not eat from any tree in the garden'?" (The word *really* is placed in the serpent's mouth in the translation of the NIV and the NAB and, according to Wenham, the Hebrew bears that sense. Instead of *really*, the English Standard Version uses *actually*.) It is a question that carries a slight nagging doubt. Doubt regarding God's instructions is a step toward self-autonomy and a step away from faith-directed submission to God's authority. How subtly the author paints the picture. In seeming innocence Eve carries herself a little further away from the Lordship of God. God said, "From any tree of the garden you may eat freely."

Eve responds (omitting "any" and "freely"), "From the fruit of the trees of the garden we may eat." The implication is that God somehow failed to provide as munificently as he might have.

Eve also follows Satan's way of referring to deity simply as "God," not as the LORD God. Furthermore, she adds to God's prohibition, "or touch it," something he did not say. She portrays God as somewhat harsh and repressive. Is not Eve's way our own way of misrepresenting an always good God, when we desperately want our own way at the expense of another? To bring the temptation to a close, the ever crafty serpent does not direct Eve to eat. He says that God has a selfish purpose in withholding the benefits of the tree. He is keeping back what is really best for Adam and Eve. "God knows that in the day you eat from it your eyes will be opened." The charm of the story lies in its apparent naiveté, which hides a depth of understanding of human nature. This brief account can be greatly expanded.

Acknowledging the moral force of the account, we still have to answer the question, is the account historical? One objection to its historicity hangs on supposed discrepancies between the two creation accounts.

Are the Two Accounts to Be Interpreted Alike?

"Discrepancies" between chapter 1 and chapters 2 and 3 are not difficult to find. The first account has creation accomplished in six days, the second in one day. In the first account plants appear three days before the creation of man; in the second man is created before the plants. The first account gives man the fruit of every tree for food; the second sets one tree apart as forbidden. The first has *everything* good, the second a serpent, which evidently was included in the creative act, being the very embodiment of evil. Are these discrepancies real? How can they be? This is the very Word of God.

Reasonable answers to the objections are found in the meaning of the days in Genesis 1 and in the literary style of the second account. Most of the supposed discrepancies between the first account and the second vanish if we take the days of Genesis 1 as themes of creation. The remainder are gone when we see the sense which the second account is intended to carry. The two accounts become complementary. The first is a picture of the majesty and power of the sovereign Creator who does all things well. The second is a graphic preview of all the Bible reveals concerning the nature of mankind, the broken relationships between man and God, and the divine steps taken to bring rebellious people back into a state of harmony with a loving God. Granting all of this, we are still faced with the problem of understanding the normal sense of the passage.

The basic question is, to what genre does Genesis 2:4-3:24 belong? *Genre* is a term used to classify literary works according to their particular style, form or content. We might think of writings that can be distinguished as either prose or poetry. But then poetry can be further divided into such categories as epics, odes, elegies, idylls, limericks and haiku. An epic may have content that is historic, legendary, futurist and so forth. Each is a separate genre. Prose writing may fall into legal, narrative, postulational, apocalyptic, or some other genre. Asking this question, the second creation account seems clearly to belong to a different genre than does Genesis 1. The interpretation of Genesis 2-3 is a separate issue from the interpretation of Genesis 1.

The evangelical reader is likely to ask, "But did not all of Genesis come from the pen of Moses? If so, how can Genesis 2-3 belong to a different genre from Genesis 1?"

Evangelicals usually consider that everything in the first five books of the Bible was written by Moses. They believe this to be true, since the New Testament in a number of places refers to specific passages in these five books as having come from Moses. This does not necessarily mean, however, that Moses himself wrote everything in the first five books. We may grant that Moses put the parts of Genesis together, but there is no necessary reason to believe that he did not use documents that had been in circulation before his time or long and carefully remembered oral traditions. Thinking as much does not for a moment suggest that any part of Genesis is not inspired by God. In giving us the books, God used human instrumentality. Those human instruments may have been directly and immediately inspired by God or they may have been providentially superintended in the selection of information brought to them by other means.

The different character and style of the two creation accounts strongly suggests they originated in different ways, even if they were edited, compiled, modified, abstracted, or written by Moses or by someone else. The conclusion that they were initially written by different hands appears reliable enough.[46]

Interpretation of the Account

If we can agree to this much, how do we interpret what we read in chapters 2 and 3? Many are satisfied to term the story an *allegory*, historical only in the sense that it is a picture of the history of mankind's relationship with God. Taken as an allegory, the story is a fictional narrative which has another and deeper meaning than the one which is expressed. In an allegory, such as John Bunyan's *The Pilgrim's Progress*, each character and place represents some virtue, vice or attitude of heart. Allegories are not foreign to Scripture. The story of the beloved and his vineyard in Isaiah 5:1-6 is an allegory. Under the inspiration of the Holy Spirit, an allegory can carry a significant message. The larger question is, did the author of Genesis 2-3 *intend* the account as an allegory?

The answer has to be no. In this creation account, Adam and Eve are not representatives of men and women generically, but are real people. Even though Adam means "man" and Eve means "woman," their reality is the clear intent of the author. This follows from the description of their children and the length of Adam's life in the chapters that follow.

A different approach is to treat the account as *story*. Story is simply another name for myth. Myth is an indirect way of expressing a world view through an account that is easily remembered and passed on. The myths of ancient Sumeria, Babylonia and Egypt were religious ways to account for the disharmonious appearance of the world. These myths have no semblance to historical reality. A different kind of myth is closely related to allegory. In an allegory the separate characters are each representative of something. In myths such as those in *Aesop's Fables,* it is the story itself that carries a useful moral teaching. Although to most of us "myth" is incompatible with the truth of God's Word, myth is clearly present in the story that Jotham told of the olive tree, the fig tree, the vine and the bramble in Judges 9:7-15. The question is, can Genesis 2-3 be counted as myth or story?

Again, we have to answer no. God, Adam, and Eve represent themselves. The succeeding chapters plainly show that Adam and Eve are considered historical personages. They have children, their children have children. They live out their lives. To be sure, the narrative conveys some powerful moral truths, as many myths are intended to do, but the account can convey moral truth without falling into the myth genre.

Is it poetry? No. Although it includes some poetry in 2:23 and 3:14-19, it is mostly written in a narrative style. Hebrew poetry is characterized by parallel lines and corresponding patterns of thought. The parallel lines are lacking except for the verses listed.

Is it then direct history? People of God through the centuries have certainly considered it so. If literal history, one must admit it is crowded with difficulties. The most obvious have to do with the serpent. Who or what is this creature? A literal, four-limbed progenitor of snakes, one that could talk and afterward was reduced to limblessness? There is nothing in the text to suggest such a creature. Or is the serpent another name for an embodied Satan, as most Christian expositors have thought? If so, how is Satan now crawling in the dust? Then we have the man and the woman hearing the footfalls of God walking in the garden. Hearing, the guilty man and woman "hid themselves from the presence of the LORD God." Can someone hide from God? This reads as if God is spatially located and delimited. Critics treat this as an expression of a primitive belief in a God who had a human form, a belief held about the gods by pagan people living in Palestine, Egypt and Mesopotamia in the days of Moses. As Christians, we know that God does not have a human form, since Scripture presents him as both invisible and omnipresent in the world. Could this rather be a pre-incarnate form of the Son of God? That such a concept was in the mind of the author and its first readers is quite improbable, but the Christian who treats every detail as literal history has to find some such explanatory device.

Still another problem is that of the insoluble geography of Eden. Where are the four rivers flowing from a single source? Some have argued that the geography was altered in the Noachian flood so that the rivers are not now located where they once were. The problem with this is that two of the rivers, the Tigris and the Euphrates, both extant rivers, are named. Did they retain their geographic identity in the Flood but the other two got washed away? Another suggestion is that Eden was below the present day sea level in what is now the Persian Gulf. This is not unbelievable, if Eden existed at a time before the end of the last ice age, when a much larger amount of the earth's water would have been entrapped in the polar ice caps and in glaciers. Emptying into the Persian Gulf south of the mouths of the Tigris and Euphrates are two wadies, one from the east and one from the west. With major climate changes during the ice age, these may have been substantial rivers. Their Biblical names, Pishon and Gihon, can perhaps be traced back to the Sumerian names for these wadies. This would account for the four rivers watering Eden, but not for their stated origin from a single source in Eden. These are but a few of the problems.

If one must take the chapters as ordinary narrative history, it would seem almost impossible to assent to the notion that man's physical body was the product of evolution, whether Darwinian evolution or evolution directed by God. Some serious Bible scholars who cannot escape evidences for an old earth (progressive creationists) accept it as narrative history and therefore insist that the physical bodies of Adam and Eve were created separately from the rest of the animal world. Russell Maatman, who competently defends progressive creationism, argues that mankind cannot have descended from animals.[47] On the basis of Genesis 2 and 3, belief in the direct creation of man by God he says is "nonnegotiable." It is an objective teaching of the Bible significant enough that for the Christian it needs to override a contradictory scientific conclusion. With all the difficulties, the question is, should the chapter be taken as narrative history?

It is entirely possible the story belongs to some genre that is different than narrative history, different than poetry, different than allegory, different than myth. To look at the issue fairly, we first need to consider the *structure* of the narrative.

Structure of the Account

Although the account reads as if it is an artless, almost childlike recitation of events, it is marked by a careful and elegant chiastic structure. It consists of a series of seven scenes. Except for the central scene, each scene corresponds in a number of ways to another one of the scenes. The correspondences form the following structure:

A_1. Narrative God the sole actor: man present but passive (2:5-17)

B_1. Narrative God main actor, man minor role, woman and animals passive (2:18-25) C_1. Dialogue Snake and woman (3:1-5)

D. Narrative Man and woman (3:6-9)

C_2. Dialogue God, man and woman (3:9-13)

B_2. Narrative God main actor, man minor role, woman and snake passive (3:14-21)

A_2. Narrative God sole actor: man passive (3:22-24)[48]

The correspondences are more detailed than is apparent from the outline alone. Sections A_1 and A_2 have a distinctive vocabulary. Only in these do we find the phrases, "on the east," "tree of life," "garden of Eden," "till," and "guard."

Scenes B_1 and B_2 are concerned with relationships between man and the rest of creation. The B_1 is the ideal: the animals were created to be man's companions, and woman is his perfect partner. B_2 corresponds to this in that it pictures the actual present situation. There is perpetual conflict between man and the serpent and relations between the sexes are far from harmonious. At the same time, both sections assert the supremacy of God the creator. Below God in a descending order we have man, whose superiority to the animals is indicated by his giving them names. At the next level in the hierarchy is woman. Man's authority over her is implied in naming her (both sections). She is plainly superior to the animals, for only she is a perfect match for man. Both scenes end with statements about woman's role as wife and mother.

In C_1 the serpent and the woman make three comments about the tree. In C_2, corresponding to this, God puts three questions to the man and his wife.

Scene D has no counterpart. It is the crux of the entire narrative. Here is the awful act of rebellion against God. The serpent is not present. God is not present. Man and woman are acting alone in justifying themselves in their deed of disobedience and are alone in the realization of what they have done.

If the author consciously developed the narrative in what is an exceptionally elaborate structure, it must be that he had a different purpose in mind than a simple recitation of historical events. Does that mean the account is not inspired? No, but it means that God was using the wisdom and art of the human author to emphasize some momentous truths. Does the literary design of the passage mean that it is not history? Again no, but it does lead us to look at it as a work of a different genre from ordinary historical narratives such as those of the books of Joshua, Judges, Ruth, I and II Samuel.

In addition to the structure, other features of the story ought to persuade the reader to take it as a different kind of literary writing. It can hardly be thought of as theological discourse. The picture is theologically correct but not theologically propositional. Propositional writing is literature that makes straightforward declarations of things that are believed to be true. For a short example, when Jesus visited with the woman at the well, as recounted in John 4, he said, "God is a Spirit." This is a plain propositional statement about God. The circumstances called for an unmistakable affirmation about God to correct an error entertained by the Samaritan woman. If Jesus was correct, we cannot think God really has a humanlike body, or that he walks and his walking issues in the sound of footfalls. The Epistle to the Romans is an example of propositional writing. Here the Apostle Paul makes a series of direct statements concerning God's plan of redemption and salvation. The account in Genesis 2:4 - 3:24 is clearly not in the same genre as Romans. In fact, the narrative cannot be taken literally without entertaining contradictory notions about God.

Nevertheless, it must be recognized there are things about God that cannot be described in propositional language. God is ineffable, inscrutable, beyond understanding except as he chooses to reveal himself to mankind. Here is a revelation he has given of himself, but it is a revelation that cannot be encapsulated in the precise language of engineers, lawyers, theologians or philosophers. Instead it is a picture that is designed to be felt and sensed.

With exceptional Spirit-directed discrimination, the human author has given us a vision of a God who genuinely desires fellowship with men and women. At the same time he is a God with whom man cannot trifle. In keeping with his character as God, he cannot continue in fellowship with a self-indulgent rebel. Yet it is also a picture of a compassionate God. The story prophetically points to a way back into harmony with God, a way that will come through a future offspring of the woman who will "crush the head" of the serpent.

The Surprising Genre

If the account is not poetry, is not allegory, is not myth, and cannot be taken as ordinary historical narrative, how is it to be understood? To what genre does it belong? It appears to have no parallel in Biblical literature or even in ancient non-biblical Semitic literature. It is a powerful but unique kind of writing given by the Spirit of God to convey an all-important prefatory message for the revelation about to be unfolded in the rest of Scripture.

Although there is no known literary parallel in the Hebrew language, a possible analogy is found in the Book of The Revelation. Revelation 12 illustrates what is found throughout the book. In this chapter are literal persons: first God; secondly the man-child, who is to rule all nations with a rod of iron and who was caught up to God and to his throne; thirdly Michael and his angels; finally a remnant "who keep the commandments of God and bear testimony to Jesus." Then there are two other major players. One is a woman clothed with the sun, the moon under her feet, and upon her head a crown of twelve stars. We are not expected to take this as a literal representation of some astronomically large woman. As we read, we discover the woman is a figure of the nation of Israel, through which the man-child came. Another player is a great red dragon with seven heads and ten horns. This is not a literal likeness of some monstrous seven-headed reptile. Verse 9 identifies this beast as a representation of "that old serpent, called the Devil, and Satan." In verse 13 the woman is given two wings of an eagle to escape the persecution of the red dragon. We most certainly do not consider the wings as literal eagle wings. What kind of writing is all this? It is not poetry. It is not allegory, since most of the characters represent themselves. It is not myth, since it is obviously intended to represent factual events in history and prophecy. It is prophetic writing, a still different genre from history, allegory, poetry, myth and propositional writing. It is writing often termed apocalyptic.

Does it not follow that Genesis 2-3 is almost the same kind of genre? We might think of it as "prophecy in reverse," prophecy looking backward toward mankind's beginning rather than forward toward days to come. The characters are real persons, yet many of the details are to be understood in a metaphorical sense. Both the characters and the details are to be taken in a sense *normal* to its unique genre. God is indeed God in chapters 2-3, although his physical walking is representative. Is his voice representative or were there physical sound waves impinging on the ears of Adam and Eve? This is something no one can answer, although it must be acknowledged that God can clearly place his words in the mind of someone, without resorting to the creation of physical sound waves. Likewise Adam and Eve are to be taken as real persons, as indicated by what follows in Genesis 4.

Perhaps the most difficult issue with this interpretation is how one is to take the serpent. The mental image created by the story is that of a literal snake, and no doubt this is the impression the author intended to produce. Is it a physical snake? The problem of treating it as a physical snake is that snakes are part of God's creation, which he pronounced "good." The serpent, however, is determined to disrupt the peace of God's creation. It is not a being given to goodness. Furthermore, it is incredible that a mere animal, however crafty, could know all the serpent here knows. The serpent even knows the hidden purposes of God. This knowledge is evident, since the serpent is inciting Adam and Eve against God.

Many Christian commentators consider the serpent to be a literal snake that Satan took over to serve his evil purposes. This interpretation follows from Satan being termed "that old serpent" in Revelation 12. Prior to the temptation the serpent was some kind of being without a resemblance to a snake, but in consequence of the temptation was consigned to crawl in the dust. Such an interpretation is fraught with obvious difficulties. Should insensate snakes be consigned to the life of a snake because of the choice of a serpent by the Devil? Zoologists might ask, "Which species of snake?" Are all known 2,500 species of snakes somehow "suffering" for the misfortune of one? There must be a better and richer understanding.

Some expositors have considered the snake with his questions to represent the stream of thoughts coursing through the mind of Eve. The craftiness of the serpent is the cunning of Eve herself. How better would one graphically picture self-justifying excuses to do wrong? The thoughts may well have been placed in her mind by Satanic suggestion. Standing in opposition to this is the curse directly addressed to the serpent by God. The author is treating the serpent as a personal, sentient being.

It is possible the author was not concerned with the identity of the snake. Who or what the snake represents could have been secondary to the progress of Eve's self-deception. In the wisdom of God, however, the snake was intentionally destined to become a figure of the Tempter, the great arch-enemy of God. This is not unreasonable in the historical context of the passage, although not necessary to the interpretation.

Passing from the problem of the serpent we also need to ask, are the tree of life and the tree of the knowledge of good and evil intended to be understood as material trees? It is entirely possible that neither was the author concerned with this question. The issue was not about material trees but about genuine choices. Not infrequently Scriptures use trees as similes of the life of God (e.g., Psalm 1:3; Jeremiah 17:8). In Proverbs 3:18 a tree of life is a metaphor of the wisdom that comes from God. In Proverbs 15:4 a tree of life is a metaphor for a wholesome tongue. In Revelation 2:7 there is a promise that, "To him who overcomes" Jesus "will grant to eat of the tree of life, which is in the Paradise of God." Quite plainly the latter is a figure of eternal life granted to the one who is a believer in the Lord Jesus Christ. (See the comment by the author of The Revelation in 1 John 5:4-5). The tree of life, whether literal or figurative, plainly enough, is a symbol for the life of God and the wisdom that resides in that life.

The significance of the *tree of good and evil* is a little more difficult to establish, since it is found only in this story.[49] The expression "good and evil" itself is uncommon in the Old Testament. With respect to its significance for the tree, its use in Deuteronomy 1:39 is suggestive. God is recounting the failure of the Israelites to enter Canaan at Kadesh-barnea. Because of their willful lack of confidence in God, they were consigned to wandering in the wilderness until that generation had died off. Of that generation only Caleb and Joshua were to be allowed to enter the land. But the children, grown after the forty years of wandering, would be allowed to enter, "children, who this day have no knowledge of good or evil." It is hard to believe these now grown children did not know right from wrong. That cannot be the meaning of the expression. What it must mean is that the children were not practicing *moral autonomy*. Unlike the king of Tyre and unlike their parents, they were not presuming to place their knowledge above that of God or to make decisions apart from God. This can well be the ultimate meaning of the tree of good and evil in the creation story. It portrays the choice of self-will, of moral autonomy.

Could the trees be literal and nevertheless carry the same moral force? Of course. But it is not necessary to the point of the story, to the doctrinal significance of the story, or even to the full inspiration of the story that they be physical trees.

Other details of the narrative can be analyzed, but with the same results. The story belongs to a kind of prophetic genre that might be termed *creation prophecy*. "Retrospective apocalypse" is what Claude Tresmontant insightfully termed it.[50] It is history written not in terms of geography and dates, but in moral and ethical metaphors. In this literary genre, the picture of the creation of Adam from the dust of the earth and Eve from his rib do not *necessarily* require an instantaneous molding of Adam's body, nor a surgical exercise on the part of God. To press the story in this way is to overlook the nature of the genre and to miss the deep truth the story intends to convey.[51]

After reading this, one might conclude that I am about to water down the truths of the creation accounts with the purpose of introducing full-blown evolution as a Biblical doctrine. Not in the least. A Christian might conclude that evolution was God's method of creation, but the concept cannot be derived from the Bible. *Genesis is simply not concerned with how God brought man's body into being.* The second and third chapters are concerned with the relationship of a man to his wife, with man's need of obedience to God, and with the awful consequences of putting one's personal desires and judgments above that of God's.

Where can a Christian find information concerning the origin of man as a physical being? How can an earnest seeker know God's truth concerning the physical history of the world and its incredible variety and numbers of living things? In large part this will have to come from another book God has given us, the very world in which we live, the world that came from his almighty hand. What does this book tell us? What has it told me? Before answering, we need to look at some other creation passages that perhaps make evolutionary doctrine totally inconsistent with sound Biblical faith. Many Christian writers insist they do. The question is, do they? The next chapter explores this question.

CHAPTER 4

OTHER CREATION PASSAGES OF CONCERN

An almost countless number of passages throughout the Bible honor and glorify God as the Creator. The deity, prior existence, and creatorship of the Lord Jesus is affirmed in Hebrews 1:2 and John 1:3. Colossians 1:15-16 declares that everything was created in, through, and for the Son of God. The collective significance of all the creation passages is forcefully summarized in Psalm 95:6.

Come, let us worship and bow down,

Let us kneel before the LORD, our Maker.

Since he is the Creator, he is to be worshiped in humility of soul. Mankind, before all else, has a solemn obligation to acknowledge him as Creator. As Creator, he commands our adoration and obedience.

The question of interest is whether any Biblical passage constrains us to accept a view that the earth and its inhabitants were created in six literal, sequential days perhaps less than 10,000 years ago. Or do Biblical passages allow us to believe that the earth is old but require a belief that all life came through a number of distinct, creative acts, as asserted by those who subscribe to the idea of progressive creation? Perhaps the Scriptures teach that God providentially superintended a creative process of evolution. Is it possible they point to a view that God initially created the world with a built-in self-ordering capacity?

God the Absolute Creator

Going beyond the first three chapters of Genesis, what do other passages of the Bible teach us about God's creative work?

Unquestionably one after another declares the creatorship of God. At the same time, when examined objectively, *none is definitive for one or another of the clearly theistic creationist views.* They state that God is responsible for creation without indicating how or when creation took place. Are there any exceptions? If any passage appears to give the lie to this assertion, it is Psalm 33:8-9.

Let all the earth fear the LORD,

Let all the inhabitants of the world stand in awe of Him!

For He spoke, and it was done;

He commanded and it stood fast.

Surely these words state that nothing less than a spoken command from God sufficed to bring creation into instant maturity. If God brought the myriad life forms into being by a gradual process, then how could it have been by a spoken command? Yet if one recalls, there were six commands in Genesis 1 that brought the earth to perfection. The psalmist was not ignorant of this. What ways then can we interpret this striking passage? It is quite possible that the one command could be a figure of speech known to grammarians as a *synecdoche*, here an instance of putting one command for six creative commands. On the other hand, it may not be a synecdoche. It may just as well stand for the great initial command implied in Genesis 1:1. As a third possibility, it could be a general and unspecified affirmation of the power of God who Himself was totally responsible for every aspect of creation. For us frail mortals, the important thing is to acknowledge with fear and awe the powerful majesty of Almighty God. With regard to the details of creation, the passage is too indecisive for anyone to build from it a doctrine of the time and manner of creation.

There is a host of verses declaring that God is the creator of mankind. The familiar Psalm 100:3 is an example:

Know that the LORD Himself is God!

It is He who has made us, and not we ourselves;

we are His people and the sheep of his pasture.

Amen! But reading and believing this averment of God's creatorship does not necessarily require that God created man and all other creatures within a literal week. There is nothing here about when or how or how long. Man's body could have been created by God's direction over a great span of time. Just as much, so far as Biblical words can be read, man's entire being, body as well as spirit, may have been created through a divine command at a specific point in time. With regard to the time and duration of creation, this and similar passages are silent except for the decisive truth that man came from the mighty hand of God.

A fact worth reflecting upon is that a number of verses speak of God *creating each individual* (Job 10:8-13; Psalm 119:73; Proverbs 22:2; Isaiah 44:2; and others). This we believe. Yet individuals are created through a complex process of differentiation and development controlled by enzymes defined by DNA molecules. Where is God's hand in the creation of the individual? It is there, since in his omniscience, omnipresence and omnipotence every atomic event must be under his supervision. Granting as much, cannot we also grant that God may have chosen to create the world with its multiplicity of life forms over a long period of time? Is creation over a period of time, whether over nine months or four-and-a-half billion years less an act of creation than instant creation through a spoken word? Why cannot the same stated function of creatorship be applied to a process God used in creating mankind as to the process for the creation of each individual's body? If the first human came into existence through an ages-long, God-directed, creative *process*, is God somehow less in control, or is his creatorship somehow diminished? God may, in fact, have made the world through six great commands a bare six thousand years ago, but a recent, abrupt creation is not necessarily a greater demonstration of his power than his intimate involvement in an ages-long process.

Mark 10:6 appears to be one of two New Testament exceptions that puts a time limit on creation. It has been used in a number of young-earth creationist books to take old-earthers to task.[52] It reads: "But from the beginning of creation, *God* MADE THEM MALE AND FEMALE." This sounds as if they were made male and female at the time of creation itself. If so, Adam and Eve had to be created simultaneously with all the great dinosaurs, the huge titanotheres, the amblypods, the shelled *Glyptodon*, the fifty-five foot long *Basilosaurus* and the thousands of other now extinct animals. This is the view of most young-earth creationists. They teach that a pair of each of the many kinds of now extinct animals were taken onto the ark and survived the flood, but became extinct some time after the flood. This passage seems to confirm such a doctrine. But this is to read into the passage more than was ever intended by these words of Jesus.

Weymouth's *New Testament in Modern Speech* brings out the sense of the passage accepted by a great many Greek scholars:

...but from the beginning of the creation the rule was, "MALE AND FEMALE DID GOD MAKE THEM. FOR THIS REASON A MAN SHALL LEAVE HIS FATHER AND MOTHER AND SHALL CLING TO HIS WIFE, AND THE TWO SHALL BE ONE."

What the passage is saying is plain. God's *intention* from the beginning was that a man should not divorce his wife, but that every marriage should endure. The verse says nothing about *when* man was created with reference to the rest of God's creation.

The other apparent New Testament exception is found in 1 Corinthians 11:8-9. The RSV places the verses in a parenthesis, translating them:

(For man was not made from woman, but woman from man.

Neither was man created for woman, but woman for man.)

This seems to confirm the commonly accepted understanding of Genesis 2 that man's physical body was immediately created by a command of God, and that Eve's body was made directly from Adam's. It seems to provide Scriptural support for the position of young-earth and many other creationists that whatever method God may have used for creation of the rest of the animal world, mankind came immediately from the hand of God. The problem is, the Greek of verse 8 does not include the word "made." It reads simply, "For man is not from woman, but woman from man." The verb is not "made" but "is." Editors of the translation assumed that "made" is what Paul had in mind. The NIV translates verse 8 differently: "For man did not come from woman but woman from man." This interprets "is" to mean, "come from." It allows the reader to think that Eve came from Adam's rib but is vague enough that it does not really mandate it. What did the Holy Spirit have in mind?

Verse 12 does not clarify matters. It literally reads, "For just as the woman [is] from (*ek*) the man, so also the man is through (*dia*) the woman; but all things [are] from God." The words imply or at least allow the thought that both here and in verse 8 this is what the Apostle Paul had in mind: the female is made through the procreative activity of the male in the same sense that the male is born through a woman. In any event, the context shows that the passage is not about God's creative work! It is intended to provide some information on whether or not a woman should have her head covered. Reading the words separated by a great span of time and culture, we don't know precisely what Paul had in mind by the woman having her head "covered" or "uncovered" while praying or prophesying. Expositors have proposed a number of answers.[53] The supposition that this passage teaches man was created simultaneously with the dinosaurs hangs on a very, very large ambiguity.

One might be firmly persuaded that God did in fact bring man's physical body into being through an ages-long, supervised process. No passage could be used to refute the concept, not even Psalm 100:3. On the other hand, no passage supports such a concept. The Scriptures tell us nothing except that whatever came into being came through the hand of God.

Suffering and Death

Numerous passages of Scripture deal with the problem of human suffering and death. Although the passages are not directly related to creation, young-earth creationists presume the passages limit the time when creation could have occurred. If suffering and death were unknown before man's fall into sin, then the death of now extinct animals found as fossils could not have occurred prior to the creation of mankind.

The Genesis account relates that when the first humans deliberately sinned, God drove them out of the Garden and announced the punishment that should follow. A life of toil, hardship and suffering followed by death would thenceforth be their expectation. To this account, young agers add the doctrine that *animal* predation, suffering and death also began with the sin of man and are consequences of the fall. They reason that since the Bible definitely teaches that all death came through the fall, evolution can only be false. If one accepts evolution, then one must give up all thought of God, or at least a loving and merciful God, for a loving God would not allow suffering and death except as a judgment upon sin. Such appears to be a reasonable and even necessary conclusion as one considers the following four supposedly definitive lines of Biblical thought. Looking at each, however, there is a reasonable alternative interpretation.

1. Genesis 1:30 says that to all land animals, every bird and all creatures crawling on the ground, God had "given every green plant for food." If only plants were given for food, death following animal predation must have been unknown.

Verse 30 reads as if every kind of animal was created able and obliged to feed solely on plants for food. The verse, of course, creates problems for every theory of creation that depends on the Biblical text. Young-earth and reconstruction creationists, who believe that before the fall every animal was an herbivore, have to explain how spiders, centipedes, frogs, cobras, shrikes, robins, kinglets, bats, pumas and thousands of other creatures abruptly had their external and internal anatomy altered from an herbivorous to a predatory structure. Advocates of progressive creation, providential creation, and macrotheistic creation (insofar as they depend on the text) have to explain what to do with this passage. Finding a harmonious explanation of the text seems less difficult than explaining a sudden, miraculous modification of God's initial creation, a modification nowhere mentioned or implied by Scripture.

The author of the passage was likely intending to generalize rather than specify what every single species of animal used for food. A large number of arthropods, amphibians, reptiles, birds, and mammals are dependent on plants at least part of the time. There are notable exceptions, of course. Ultimately, all life except for some of the simplest bacteria is dependent on energy supplied by green plants. This is the role of photosynthesis carried out by plants. This modern understanding can hardly be thought to have been known to the author. The statement in Genesis 1:30 may be intended to say no more than that through the wonderful creation of plants God made adequate provision of food for his creatures. Animal predation is not at issue in the text.

2. Paul stated in Romans 5:12 that man's sin was the cause of death. Could this mean there was no death prior to Adam's disobedience? Yet Romans 5:12 is obviously concerned only with human death. The second half of Romans 5:12 reads, "and so death spread to all men, because all sinned." It is gratuitous to read animal death into Paul's discussion.

3. 1 John 4:8, as well as other passages, asserts that God is love. This is one of his basic moral attributes. It appears reasonable to assume that before the fall a loving God would not have countenanced the cruel destruction of a hapless, squealing chipmunk in the jaws of a hungry coyote. The suffering of a chipmunk and countless other millions of organisms in a presumed process of evolution is unworthy of God, it is claimed, unless suffering was caused by sin.

This objection founders when we ask, "Why then at the *present* time would God will the painful death of a chipmunk because of the *sin of man*?" Did God abandon his loving concern for the animal world when man sinned? Furthermore, if God has this concern for the animal world, it is strange that God directed animal sacrifices under the Mosaic law. These included sacrifices for sin, but also included worship sacrifices of essentially all animals used for food (animals taken in the hunt were excluded from the necessity of being presented as an offering).

There is no question but that all *human* suffering is traceable to sin, at least as far as Scripture is concerned. By no means is all suffering the *direct* result of sin. That was the theological error of Job's comforters. They could not understand Job's suffering without assuming that in some respect unknown to them Job had been a grievous transgressor. The point of the Book of Job as well as of many other Scriptures is that God uses human suffering in different ways, but always out of a necessity imposed by sin. Suffering for some is a kindness leading them to seek relief in God's grace. For others it is a judgment upon evil. For believers it may be a vehicle of correction. Paul found his suffering a means God was using to instruct him in an understanding of grace. To refer any of these things to the animal world goes beyond what is written or what we are competent to understand.

4. Romans 8:18-22 definitely seems to requires a sentence of destruction on the earth following the fall of man. Natural evil, it appears, did not precede the fall. This is the strongest textual argument for the absence of sin and death prior to the creation and fall of man. It is worth reproducing these verses in their context (deleting the verse numbers).

> For I consider that the sufferings of this present time are not worthy to be compared with the glory that is to be revealed to us. For the anxious longing of the creation waits eagerly for the revealing of the sons of God. For the creation was subjected to futility, not of its own will, but because of Him who subjected it, in hope that the creation itself also will be set free from its slavery to corruption into the freedom of the

glory of the children of God. For we know that the whole creation groans and suffers the pains of childbirth together until now. And not only this, but also we ourselves, having the first fruits of the Spirit, even we ourselves groan within ourselves, waiting eagerly for *our* adoption as sons, the redemption of our body.

What is the Apostle saying? Where this translation from the NASB has the word *creation*, the Authorized (King James) Version has the word *creature*. Both versions represent interpretations of their translators. By itself the word may legitimately be translated either *creature* or *creation*. By using *creature* the AV makes the passage speak only of human beings. The word *creature* is used in the sense of humans in general. If this is the correct way to read the passage, and there are a few expositors who think it is, the verses have nothing to say about suffering and death in the animal world.

Most modern translations and expositors, however, choose the word *creation*, which makes the passage speak about the whole earth, not just mankind. *Creation* seems to be required by the sense of the passage as a whole.[54]

Presuming that Paul is writing about broader aspects of creation than mankind alone, what does the passage require us to understand? Paul's major point is that we who are believers, groaning and suffering as we do in this life, have an incredibly glorious prospect ahead of us. In a stunning act of God's power and grace we are going to be raised from the dead! Our very bodies, subject as they now are to every ill and injury and finally to death, are going to be redeemed. We who believe have the evidence within ourselves: "the first fruits of the Spirit."

The rest of creation "waits eagerly for the revealing of the sons of God." In a delightful figure of speech, Paul treats creation as if it has a mind and can wait and wish with us for that great day when God's power will transform and reveal the Christian for all he or she really has become in union with Christ. At that time creation itself will be set free and will be transformed. Creation will obtain "the freedom of the glory of the children of God."

The promise that creation in some way will be transformed, can only mean that in some very real sense creation today is not what God ultimately plans for it. "Creation was subjected (at some time in the past) to futility" and now is "in slavery to corruption." What is Paul getting at? Is there some deeper meaning to the word *futility*? The Greek lexicon of Bauer, Arndt, and Gingrich says that in this verse the word (*mataiotes*) means "frustration."[55] As other possible translations they list "emptiness, futility, purposelessness, transitoriness." The range of meanings lacks specificity. It is difficult to get more out of the word than that creation in some way is far from what God wants it to be or what it ultimately will be. What does *slavery to corruption* mean? The word *corruption* (*phthoras*) may mean ruin, destruction, dissolution, deterioration, decay. In some way the world is the slave of either corruption or destruction, or it is enslaved to dying. This is the present state of things. Undoubtedly it was what the Apostle Paul repeatedly observed as he trudged along Roman roads on his missionary journeys. He would have seen crops ravaged by insects, forests burnt by fires, vultures circling in the sky over the carcass of an animal killed by a lion, fierce storms smashing fishing boats against rocky shores, livestock weakened and often dying from disease, creation not at peace but hostile and warring. The question is, how did creation get that way?

We cannot answer how creation came to be hostile and warring until we ask *when* it became that way. Two possibilities stand out. (a) The sin of man made it so. At the point of Adam's sin all creation suddenly went awry. Formerly peaceful herbivores were transformed into fierce carnivores. Whatever food leopards, eagles, hawks, flycatchers, sea gulls, pythons, sharks, ticks, scorpions, tiger beetles, and other predators enjoyed before this event, they now turned to living prey. Thousands of species of once innocuous and harmless roundworms, flatworms and protozoans suddenly became malign parasites. We can't exclude any death-dealing organisms from the picture, not even spiders that spin webs to trap insect prey. This possible explanation, one must admit, stretches credulity to the breaking point and casts serious doubt on the young-earth view. (b) It is possible that creation, *originally constituted with a degree of emptiness or transitoriness, was made less than what it will become in the earthly kingdom of glory.* This interpretation says that creation was filled with carnivores and parasites, was racked by storms and fires, and was subject to catastrophes before Adam ever came on the scene. This second option, however, poses a different kind of problem. Would God have made creation in any way less than perfect? How do we choose between these possible interpretations?

Whichever view we take, this uncomfortable fact remains: there is nothing, absolutely nothing, in the text itself that tells how or when creation became filled with terror and death. Those expositors who have said it was all the result of Adam's sin have read *into* the text their belief that God would not have created swallows, robins, tigers, dragonflies, octopuses, tarantulas, toads, whales and thousands of other species of animals as predators. God would have been obligated to create them all as plant-eaters.

Those expositors who consider that creation had most of its present characteristics prior to Adam can easily enough argue that under the providential hand of God, creation was perfect at every stage of its ages-long development. Every stage represented *a stage of becoming*. A fetus in the womb is perfect in a true sense, yet the fetus is not what it will be after its birth, and even then far from what it will be upon attaining maturity.

But then in what way will creation be "set free from its bondage to decay"? Will it evolve into something different? The answer is implied in the passage and is clearly stated elsewhere in the Bible. The liberation will be at a specific point, the time when we ourselves receive the "adoption," that is, the time of our resurrection. For creation as well as for us there will be an abrupt and sweeping conversion, a total metamorphosis of all nature. "The new heavens and the new earth" inaugurated by the King of Kings at his glorious return will constitute that final and perfect freedom.[56]

This important section of Romans presents the most heartening and sublime hope for the future both for the individual believer and for the world. It does not, however, unequivocally specify how the world came to be the way it is. Death and decay are a fact of life both for the Christian and for creation. Yet the time is coming, possibly is even near at hand, when the Son of David will return with all the power of heaven itself to establish his kingdom, and reign over all mankind and all creation.

Some strong inferences

What is the real basis for the current storm of dogmatic pronouncements within evangelicalism over the mode and time of creation? Ostensibly it is in defense of the authenticity of the Word of God, but one cannot help but wonder. What is being defended? In most instances it is an unbelievable scenario which demands that Tyrannosaurus, Triceratops, Brontosaurus, Stegosaurus, Pteranodon, Tillotherium, the elephant-size Pyrotheres, the saber-toothed tigers and thousands of other now extinct animals be created the same week as humans, and further supposes all these beasts to have been shipmates on the ark. Nevertheless, Biblical faith is not defended in the least by demanding an interpretation not at all *required* by Scripture.

The young-earth view could be correct, as far as Scripture alone, uninformed by science, is concerned. Some modification of the reconstruction plot may be true, although it seems difficult to support the view as usually proposed. Just as truly, neither do Scriptures forbid the progressive creationist view. Neither is the providential creationist view forbidden, at least if we look fairly at the difficulties involved in taking the second creation account as narrative history and choose to read it as "retrospective apocalypse." If we are fair, we are bound to recognize there are reasonable ways of reading the creation accounts based on Biblically justifiable principles of interpretation that permit the concept of an old earth. The same principles seem to allow the *possibility* of the creation of man's physical body through an ages-long, divinely guided process with mankind as an authentic spiritual being created in the image of God through a special act bestowed on Adam and Eve.

Where does this leave us? Is the following thought altogether too shocking to contemplate? God may have left us free and even responsible to make our own informed judgments regarding his time and method of creation. Matters that are truly important for beings created "in the image of God" have indeed been spelled out with no little precision. Tangential issues are left to human minds, not minds blind to God, but minds endowed by God himself with the faculty of reason and an obligation to approach creation with understanding and reverential respect.

What then is decisive? The scientific evidence cannot be ignored. Science does not determine our interpretation of Scripture, but in the absence of a clear Biblical pronouncement regarding God's choice of a creative method, science can well give us needed direction. Some things that science clearly shows us follow.

CHAPTER 5

HAS GOD REVEALED HIS METHOD OF CREATION?

Are there compelling evidences that all organisms have had a common ancestry? For those who want to look, there are evidences most difficult to deny. By this I do not mean evidences for a process of evolution that lacked God's direction. Although there is a staggering array of evidences for believing in descent from a common ancestor, the evidences by no means prove that Darwin's unplanned, undirected and goal-free natural selection was responsible.

One volume cannot begin to list and explain all the arguments for evolution. The most I can do is present a few particularly interesting evidences. These are evidences for which anti-evolutionists have proposed no truly satisfactory explanations.

Fossil-bearing Rocks

The fossil record is frequently advanced as providing irrefutable evidence for evolution. It is also most frequently challenged by those who are determined to give the lie to evolution. What exactly does the fossil record demonstrate?

If viewed fairly and objectively, the evidence is plain enough. Different forms of life appear in stages. Fossils of simpler forms of life first appear in older rocks, then more complex forms appear in younger rocks. The sequence of fossils does not by itself prove evolution. It does, however, provide a history that is compatible with the concept of evolution. It also presents problems that are inexplicable if all life was created the same week as humans with fossil-bearing rocks formed in the flood of Noah.

Anyone traveling through the mountains of the western United States cannot help but notice different kinds of rocks layered one on top of the other. The impression is that of looking at an enormous, sliced, layer cake. How did the rocks come to be arranged in such layers? Unless they were created fully formed, one layer above the other, they must by some means or another have been deposited in sequence. Each layer is a stratum. Just as a chef constructing a cake must put one layer on the bottom before applying filling and placing another on top, so we would expect the lower stratum to have been laid down first. Then sometime later the next stratum of rock would have been deposited. If three strata should be visible, we would conclude that the top stratum was deposited at a still later date. Geologists term this the Law of Superposition. Its truth should be self-evident. This principle of the oldest rocks on the bottom and the most recent on top follows for all strata, unless some force drastically inverted or shifted the layers after their original formation. If they have been inverted or shifted, we should expect to find some visible evidence of it.

Could God have created at the same time all the layers pretty much as we see them? Two centuries and more ago Christian thinkers supposed so. Yet after a careful study of the rocks and a cataloguing of their fossils, the supposition became ridiculous. The rocks plainly exhibit a history. Is not this a history that God has left for human study and contemplation? If the history never existed, if it is a fiction, then God is deceiving us. Yet the Bible constantly presents God as absolutely truthful. He is without the least shadow of guile or deviousness. Can any Christian prefer a God of falsehood to a God who left a truthful record for our very eyes?

Of the many different kinds of rocks that are found, geologists recognize three major categories. *Igneous* rocks are formed by the cooling and crystallization of melted rock. *Sedimentary* rocks may result from the accumulation of solid materials carried by wind or water to a place of deposition. Sedimentary rocks may also be formed through chemical action, the way limestones, dolomite, evaporites and chert are formed. A third type of rock, *metamorphic* rock, is formed when the size, shape and arrangement of the particles or crystals that compose sedimentary or other rocks are changed by heat, pressure, or solution.

Sedimentary rocks are of primary interest for this discussion, since in the process of deposition they often include remains of animals and plants that lived at the time of their formation. Sometimes these fossil remains are preserved in the rocks as silhouette-like impressions of the original organism, sometimes as trails or footprints, sometimes as complete skeletons. Occasionally fossils are imbedded in amber and are so lifelike one can suppose they perished just yesterday.

It is important to note that by the use of careful mapping, a particular stratum can be followed for hundreds of miles. Where the strata are not visible at the surface, cores taken from the earth in a search for oil and minerals aid in determining the continuity and position of a stratum. Seismic techniques also reveal the position of strata far below the surface. This is the use of man-made shock waves, created by small explosions, that travel downward into the earth. The waves reflect off different layers of rock and bounce back to the surface. The reflected waves are recorded, then converted into a cross section of the earth below the shock.

When a sequence of strata with their associated fossils is examined, each stratum may carry with it distinctly different types of fossils. Professional geologists have long observed that each type of fossil always occurs in a particular order with respect to other types of fossils. If we find type A fossil in one stratum and type B fossil in a stratum above it, wherever fossils A and B occur, type A will be lower and older and type B will lie above it and be younger. Of course, if beds are overturned, or if pressure from the collision of two, great, slowly moving surface plates (plates making up the earth's lithosphere) shoves an older stratum over a younger stratum, as sometimes happens, the younger will lie on top of the older. Where this has occurred, it is obvious after mapping the larger area. Geologists also claim that if a stratum contains a certain suite of fossils, wherever that same suite of fossils is found in strata elsewhere on the globe, those strata will be of the same general age.

Young-earth creationists counter that fossils simply do not always occur in the same order with respect to other kinds of fossils. They also contend that dating some rocks at the same age as rocks elsewhere in the world because they contain the same groups of fossils is a muddle-headed procedure. They claim the whole scheme of rock dating by fossils involves circular reasoning. Rocks are assigned a certain date because of the fossils they contain, and the fossils are given a certain relative date because geologists assume the truth of evolution. A fossil has to be a certain age because of its place in the evolutionary scheme. The evolutionary scheme is then "proved" by noting the dates of the fossils.[57]

The Grand Canyon in northwestern Arizona provides us with a remarkable slice of the earth's crust. Taken together with other formations in its environs, it displays a series of strata in the order in which they were deposited. In spite of what young-earth creationists so often claim, the sequence of fossils found in these strata has the simplest aquatic organisms at the lowest levels, with a progression to terrestrial and successively more complex organisms at the uppermost levels. Invariably, animal remains found at the lower levels are those limited to life in the water. Although there is a variety of land-dwelling forms at the upper levels, there are also both simple and complex organisms found at the upper levels. The sequence is paralleled by similar sequences in undisturbed strata around the world.

The Grand Canyon of the Colorado is worth considering in some detail, first, because many readers will likely have seen the Grand Canyon for themselves and will have an impression enabling them to visualize the discussion. Second, the strata in the canyon are fairly easy to follow, since they have not been appreciably warped by pressures within the earth or misplaced by large faults. Third, the canyon has been the focus of the best minds within the young-earth creationist movement. The Institute for Creation Research sponsors an annual tour of the canyon with options of a raft trip on the Colorado River, hiking groups on Grand Canyon Trails, and a bus tour of Northern Arizona and Southern Utah.

As we stand on the more commonly visited south rim of the canyon, we get the impression of seeing a canyon within a canyon. We view the great, spectacular, rim-to-rim expanse, from Bright Angel on the south, seven miles across to the north rim. Far below the rim is a broad floor, the Tonto Platform. Cutting through this floor is the narrow, deep, inner gorge.

In our thinking, let's take a walk down one of the canyon trails from the South Rim. A good trail may be the Kaibab Trail, which takes off from Yaki Point and ends up at the suspension foot bridge over the Colorado River near Phantom Ranch. We probably shall want to descend without much resting, then take our time examining the rocks on the way up.

Some things we shall not be able to view for ourselves, at least not without spending months in the Canyon or visiting a number of museums, are some of the interesting fossils found at many of the levels. We certainly shall not be able to determine if there are significant gaps in the fossil record. There are gaps, but these kinds of things are known only from studying thousands of specimens in museum collections. Many fossil species are rare. To compare the species, paleontologists sometimes have to visit numbers of museums where collectors have deposited their specimens.

At the bottom, perhaps where Bright Angel Creek coming from the north empties into the Colorado River, we consider the dark, lowest rocks of the inner gorge. At this point, these rocks are known as the Vishnu Metamorphic Complex. Someone taking a raft trip down the canyon will see other metamorphic and volcanic formations that make up the inner gorge. As we examine these up close, we observe they have the appearance of buried roots of an ancient mountain. They are made of sands and muds, which must have been level when they were deposited, but are now folded, bent, and metamorphosed. The original sedimentary structures were greatly altered so that they now have a different crystalline structure than they originally had. We can also see where molten masses of granite from below were forced into cracks within them.

What makes them appear to be roots of an ancient mountain range is, first of all, the fact that they are metamorphic rocks. Sedimentary or igneous rocks change into metamorphic rocks only under great heat and pressure, so these rocks must have been under a great weight of rocks above them. The weight above them was not the weight of the present layers of rock, since the pattern of folding is not continued into the rocks above.

Second, the tops of these rocks are leveled, right across the folds, bends and granitic intrusions, as if by a gigantic plane. Every appearance is that these are ancient mountains worn flat by erosion, so that only their foundations remain. There are no evidences of former life in these rocks (Fig. 1).

Above these oldest rocks we see strata of tilted rocks, which include a brilliant vermilion mud rock, a layer of cemented pebbles (conglomerate), a dark limestone, and a purple quartzite.

Collectively this is the Grand Canyon Supergroup. Preserved in the vermilion shales are asymmetrical ripple marks indicating changing currents of water, and also there are large shrinkage cracks where the mud was dried by a hot sun. The limestone in this group looks much the same as reefs being made today in other parts of the world through the activities of blue-green bacteria. It has layered, lumpy, rock masses made by the bacteria. The lumpy masses are termed stromatolites. In one important respect these Grand Canyon deposits are different from modern reefs formed by blue-green bacteria. Reefs being formed today are rife not only with blue-green bacteria but with a great many species of shellfish and other complex, multicellular organisms. These Grand Canyon rocks lack remains of any kind of shellfish or other multicellular organism. The Grand Canyon Supergroup belongs to rocks assigned to the Second Eon or the *Proterozoic*.

Climbing up the trail we note that the tilted strata of the Grand Canyon Supergroup are surmounted by more or less horizontal rocks. These are rocks of the Tonto Platform. We first come to a brown sandstone that forms the rim of the inner gorge. The size of the grains seems inconsistent with irregular sizes that would have been deposited by an enormous deluge, but is quite consistent with sands deposited near a shore. These sands in turn were topped with mud that has now turned to shale. In the shale are fossils of sea animals, some related to snails, but unlike any present day mollusk species.

Richard S. Beal, Jr.

Figure 1. Strata of the Grand Canyon. See Table 1.

Millions of years b.p.	Period	Characteristic fossils in the Grand Canyon and its environs
1840 to 540	Precambrian	Vishnu Metamorphic Complex. No fossils. Above, the Grand Canyon Supergroup with stromatolites made by blue-green bacteria.
540 to 505	Cambrian	Many phyla. Elsewhere simplest chordates.
505 to 438	Ordovician	Absent in the Grand Canyon. See text.
438 to 408	Silurian	Absent in the Grand Canyon. See text.
408 to 360	Devonian	Fishlike placoderms; brachiopods abundant
260 to 320	Mississippian	Foraminifera, crinoids, other invertebrates. Conodonts the only vertebrates in this stratum in the canyon.
320 to 280	Pennsylvanian	Fusulinids abundant. Coal beds elsewhere.
286 to 245	Permian	Tracks of various invertebrates, salamander-like animals, small reptiles. Stratum at rim is oceanic limestone with abundant corals.
245 to 208	Triassic	Remnants at rim of canyon; dinosaur tracks to east of canyon.
208 to 144	Jurassic	Extinct reptiles, oceanic deposits north, south, east of canyon.
144 to 66	Cretaceous	Large coal beds, marine deposits. Elsewhere great fossil reptiles.
66 to 1.6	Tertiary	Bird and mammal fossils east of canyon.
1.6 to present	Quaternary	Cutting of canyon begins. Bird, mammal fossils. Elsewhere human-like fossils.

Table 1

Many of the fossils are arthropods, but these arthropods are completely distinct from any arthropod existing on earth today. Arthropods are an enormous assemblage of animals that includes crabs, barnacles, insects, centipedes and spiders. These arthropods are trilobites. Some species are smaller than a fingernail, some over three inches in length. Above the shale is limestone of a kind formed at sea far out from the beach. Geologists assign these very old rocks (old because they are near the bottom of the canyon) to an age termed the *Cambrian*. Cambrian is the name given rocks elsewhere in the world exhibiting the same set of organisms.

At this point we do well to observe that no fossils of bony fish, no fossils of amphibians, and no fossils of other land-dwelling animals are ever found intermixed with fossils specific to the Cambrian period. Surely this indicates a time in history when such organisms were not yet in existence.

In many parts of the world are two successive series of rocks younger than the Cambrian but older than the next layer found in the Grand Canyon. That is, they are strata on top of the Cambrian. The older stratum, the *Ordovician*, wherever found, contains fossils of corals, trilobites, snails and animals somewhat similar to our pearly nautilus. Also present in the Ordovician layers are fish-like animals termed ostracoderms. In their anatomical structure these are most similar to our present-day lampreys and hagfish. They are unlike contemporary lampreys and hagfish in that they are covered with bony plates. They fundamentally resemble lampreys in that they lack jaws, ventral fins and scales, structures found in bony fish. Layers of rocks with these kinds of fossils do not occur in the Grand Canyon.

Some young-earth creationist writers have made much of the fact that there are missing strata in the canyon (Fig. 1). Whether we believe in evolution or not, do these missing strata provide evidence to bolster the claims of young-earth creationists? Why is a layer with such fossils – primitive invertebrates and anatomically very simple vertebrate animals - missing? Objectors say the reason is plain enough. There is no such thing in the geological record as a regular sequence of Precambrian--Cambrian--Ordovician--Silurian--etc. rocks. (See Table 1.) The sequence has been made up by geologists hell-bent on making a case for their evolutionary presuppositions.

Other possible explanations, which an honest student of creation should at least seriously consider, is that during this particular period of time the land in Northern Arizona was above sea level so that such rocks would not have been formed. Or the rocks may have been formed and eroded away after deposition. In either event, these rocks with their unique kinds of fossils would be lacking. That this is a reasonable enough explanation comes from extensive and careful geological mapping of the southwestern United States. Ocean-formed rocks with these kinds of fossils are indeed found across parts of Arizona and nearby in Southern Nevada and Southern Utah. It seems obvious that whatever ocean existed at that time simply did not cover the earth in northern Arizona, so strata of this period are lacking at the Grand Canyon. Where these ocean-formed rocks are found they are directly on top of Cambrian rocks, with no other kind of rocks or kinds of fossils in between!

Immediately on top of the Ordovician rocks in other parts of the world are rocks termed the *Silurian*. Although in North America most of the Silurian rocks are limited to the eastern United States and Canada, they are found on top of Ordovician rocks in southern Nevada and extending north into Utah, Colorado and Idaho. During this period the Grand Canyon area was manifestly still above sea level. Fish-like organisms are rare (but not totally wanting) in the Silurian beds. The Silurian does contain some other animals found in no other periods, among them a strange, four-sided coral with a cover of four limy plates (*Goniophyllum*), some other unique corals, some species of trilobites obviously different from those found in the Ordovician, and some abundant sea lilies. Sea lilies are not plants but animals. They are in the same group of animals as the starfish, the Echinodermata.

What comes next in the Grand Canyon sequence (immediately above the Cambrian rocks) may be difficult to see without getting off the trail for a bit of exploration. If adventurous enough, we would be looking for some deposits of limestone and sandstone, which must at one time have been quite extensive, but appear to have been nearly eroded away. Only isolated patches or pockets remain. They are unique for the fossils they contain. These are *Devonian* rocks, which include fossils of fish scales and plates of bony skin. Two different classes of fish occur in the Devonian. One class, which includes our sharks and rays, is represented by a number of different species of placoderms, wholly extinct today. These are recognized by scales with enamel on the outside and dentine on the inside, similar to the structure found in human teeth. Bony fish with bony scales represent another class of fish occurring in Devonian rocks. Corals, shellfish and trilobites occur in the Devonian, but *all are different species than those found in the preceding rocks*. A group of aquatic animals known as brachiopods (lamp shells) is especially common.

On top of the fragmentary Devonian rocks, about the middle level of the canyon, is a prominent and conspicuous stratum forming a great red cliff, the Redwall Limestone. This is assigned to the *Mississippian Age*. The same types of marine fossils found in these rocks are found in rocks connected to these all the way to the north through western Canada. Geologists consider this evidence that a great sea connection once existed between the area of Northern Arizona and Canada.

The stone of the Redwall is over 99 percent pure calcium carbonate. Calcium carbonate is a familiar chemical compound. Limestone, marble and chalk are all composed of calcium carbonate, as are many of the antacid mixtures we swallow. Eggshells, oyster shells, pearls and the bones of our body are mostly calcium carbonate. Where does the nearly pure calcium carbonate come from to make up Redwall Limestone cliffs? There is no great mystery about this. Calcium is present in seawater (as ions), being washed in by the rivers. Carbon dioxide is dissolved in seawater, having been produced as a by-product of respiration by animals and bacteria, and also by plants at nighttime. A great many kinds of small animals and plants combine the carbon dioxide and calcium to manufacture skeletons or shells of calcium carbonate. As the animals and plants die, their skeletons settle to the bottom to make deposits that will harden as limestone. In some instances fine needles of calcium carbonate are deposited directly from seawater. As the carbon dioxide content increases, the water will hold more calcium carbonate. But then as evaporation takes place, the calcium carbonate is precipitated to form lime muds which turn to limestone.

Geologists recognize four subdivisions of the Redwall. The lowest is the Whitmore Wash Member, the next the Thunder Springs Member, above this the Mooney Falls Member, and on top the Horseshoe Mesa Member. Fossils are rare in the Whitmore Wash Member. Invertebrate marine fossils are abundant in the Thunder Springs Member and the Mooney Falls Member. Larger marine fossils are present but rare in the Horseshoe Mesa Member, but at least sixteen species of Foraminifera are present. Foraminifers are one-celled protozoa that elaborate distinctive shells.

All species of fossils found in the Redwall are now extinct. For that matter, fossil species found in strata below the Redwall are all extinct. This is a puzzling fact, if the strata were formed at a relatively recent date. According to the flood-geology model, all species were created in the original week. Some supposedly became extinct in the flood, but some survived. Where are fossils of ones that survived? One would think at least a few would be represented in the Redwall.

How was the Redwall formed according to the flood-geology model? The young-earth geologist Stephen A. Austin accounts for the great thickness of these beds not by gradual deposition in quiet seas but by a rapid mixture of pure calcium carbonate sediments washed in from oceans to the west.[58] That the water came from the west is indicated by the greater thickness of the beds at the Nevada border and the gradual thinning of the beds at the eastern end of the canyon. The enormous wave would have wrenched bottom dwellers from the floor, combined them with swimming animals and quantities of debris and carried them (Foraminifera, brachiopods, crinoids, conodonts, gastropods, bivalves, cephalopods, blastoids, trilobites, ostracods, fish teeth and algal remains) up over the land. At the same time, these waters became hot from "the fountains of the great deep," thus precipitating the layers within days. An absolutely enormous amount of hot water would have been required, since the Redwall extends across virtually all of Northern Arizona except for the east central part of the state.

What is the evidence that a violent flood, mixed with quantities of hot water from volcanically-heated underground sources, produced the Redwall members? First, according to Austin, in one small part about twenty miles below Glen Canyon Dam are fossils of some elongated animals similar to the Chambered Nautilus. These are oriented in one direction indicating that they were in a current.[59]

Secondly, crinoid heads (animals distantly related to starfish) are sometimes found whole in the limestone. Since crinoid heads are subjected to rapid breakdown when they die, the presence of whole heads indicates rapid burial. Thirdly, inclined bedding (cross beds) has been reported at some locations, indicating deposition made by great waves, not deposition within a quiet sea. With this convincing evidence, the young-earth creationists seem to believe they have mainstream geologists backed into a corner.

Alas, it just doesn't work out this way. No doubt Dr. Austin is quite sincere in his flood geology beliefs, but he does not present the whole story. The Mooney Falls Member is the thickest member, and the one that is most apparent to visitors at the Grand Canyon. It is predominantly pure limestone, so pure that in two Arizona localities it is being mined for the manufacture of cement and lime. For the most part it simply does not show any sign of crossbedding. It has every appearance of normal deposition in a relatively quiet sea. Where the Redwall shows crossbedding is in a few places in the upper third of the member. Evidences of water currents in these places are more easily explained as the result of movements near the margins of the sea. The same explanation can account for the orientation of the fossil nautiloids that Austin observed. The supposed evidence from preservation of a few intact crinoid heads is tenuous at best. What is most remarkable and is not mentioned by Austin is that each member of the Redwall has its own distinct fossil species.

To cite some of the distinct fossils in members of the Redwall, each member is supplied with fossil conodonts. The part of conodonts so abundantly preserved in ancient strata are peculiar teeth-like structures found in the mouths of these now extinct wormlike vertebrates.[60] Each species is clearly defined by differences in the shapes of the "teeth." Conodonts with one tooth structure (*Gnathodes typicus*) are found in the Whitmore Wash Member. Two different conodonts (*Scoliognathus anchoralis* and *Dolignathus latus*) are characteristic of the Thunder Springs Member. A still different conodont (*Gnathodus texanus*) occurs in the Mooney Falls Member and the lower part of the Horseshoe Mesa Member. Yet another conodont (*Taphrognathus variarus*) is limited to the Horseshoe Mesa Member. Species of fossil Foraminifera, provide a parallel example. Different species occur in each member.[61]

Here is a great unexplained problem for flood geologists. What peculiar kind of a flood – within days – carefully sorted these fossils into their respective species, depositing one set into one layer, another set into another layer, and another into a third?

As a general principle, flood geology authors account for such sorting of similar-sized species by supposing that waves moving from different directions picked up specimens from varied ecological habitats. Is this a reasonable explanation for the different species in the members of the Redwall? No. If the Redwall was formed by one or several great waves mixing with hot water from other sources, all in a matter of days, it is incredible that no mixing of fossil species took place. In fact, it is incredible to think that the fossil species were not already well mixed, when, according to the model, enormous waves sweeping around the world already had churned the waters as they moved trillions of tons of earth to form the strata beneath the Redwall. The only reasonable explanation for the Redwall Limestone members is that they were formed in relatively quiet seas over a great span of time. If rocks anywhere show evidence of having been formed by the Noachian flood, they surely would have been formed sometime after the Redwall Limestone was deposited. These rocks and the layers below them necessarily must have antedated any possible world-wide flood.

In other parts of the United States, the Mississippian has fossils of some quite simple vertebrate animals other than conodonts. They are not impressive creatures. Their skeletons are small, salamander-like. If the Mississippian and strata above it were formed in one great universal deluge, even supposing it transported animals from restricted ecological habitats, one surely would expect some fossils more advanced than amphibians, at least a vertebra of a whale, a skull of a porpoise, or some other evidence of a reptilian, avian or mammalian denizen of the oceans.

If we happen to be reading a popular guide to the Grand Canyon by Edwin D. McKee, possibly one still sold in curio stores at the canyon, we will find no mention of the next period, the *Pennsylvanian.* Dr. McKee was an exceptionally able interpreter of the geology of the Canyon. More precise studies made since his time have clarified the status of the next rocks going up the scale, rocks of the Watahomigi Formation. These are now known to belong to the Pennsylvanian. The Pennsylvanian with its particular suite of fossils also follows the Mississippian in other parts of the United States. For that matter, the Pennsylvanian follows the Mississippian wherever it occurs in undisturbed strata elsewhere in the world. It is the period containing the enormous Appalachian, Illinois and the Mid-Continent coal fields. Associated with the Pennsylvanian coal fields are fossils of many kinds of amphibia and also insects, centipedes, spiders and scorpions. Some of the insects were remarkably large, some over a foot long.

It should be noted that no remains of winged insects are found in strata that occur *beneath* the Pennsylvanian. On the other hand, fossils of insects and other land-dwelling arthropods are not at all uncommon in strata lying *above* the Pennsylvanian.

Above these rocks are some alternating layers of quartz sandstone and red mudstone, still Pennsylvanian. What is particularly interesting about these sandstones, given our concern about how these rocks came to be, is that they are mostly made up of very thin layers, thin enough to require a hand lens for good observation. Each layer shows a grading of the sand grains from coarse to fine. There seems to be no question but that each layer is the record of a single wind ripple. They are identical to the kinds of deposits made by winds today, but are *totally unlike* anything known to be produced by flood waters.

By this time, I am exhausted and ready to devour the lunch in my knapsack and take a rest. I suspect you are too. We definitely are still within the canyon and can see a considerable climb ahead. As we examine the rocks where we stop, we find alternating layers of sandstone and shale belonging to the *Permian* period. The flood-geology view considers all these layers to have been formed by successive sweeps of the waters of the flood. Contrariwise, the geologist Ronald C. Blakey provided evidence that some are shallow marine deposits, some are wind-formed, some probably deposited by sluggish streams.[62] It is worth noting that the lowest of these layers, the Supai Group, includes some tracks of short-legged, four-footed land animals, some with three, some with four and some with five toes. Some of these are easily seen coming up the trail. What were these animals? Permian beds elsewhere include skeletons of sprawling reptiles (labyrinthodonts), some kinds of which undoubtedly made these tracks. Their tracks are in the Canyon, but their skeletons have yet to be discovered in the Canyon. What were these animals doing walking around, if it is true that everything had been violently tossed about in a gigantic world-wide flood?

Resuming our climb, we move into the Hermit Formation, also Permian. This is an accumulation of mud and fine sandy material with evidence of pools and arroyos. The wavy ripple-marks on the borders of the pools, the raindrop impressions, the numerous sun-cracks, the trails of worms, the footprints of small salamander-like animals all testify to a time of relative quiet. Was this an interlude in a world-wide flood? If so, it would seem to have been a very long interlude. Many species of plants are found fossilized in the Hermit Formation, principally ferns and small cone-bearing plants. All are of a relatively dwarf size. Interestingly, there is an absence of moist-climate and swamp-loving types. The only way of accounting for these types seems to be that when these plants were growing the region was semi-arid. This corresponds with the hardened sun cracks found in the rocks. The area was periodically covered with mud, then the mud dried out. It is extremely difficult to think that the Hermit Formation was made by a great deluge which just happened to pick up, sort, and deposit desert-type plants at this particular place, although this is what is proposed by flood geologists.

Above the Hermit Formation is the pinkish-white Coconino Sandstone. The sand is in relatively thin layers and the layers are at angles characteristic of slopes of sand dunes. Middleton, Elliott and Morales summarize the evidence that this sandstone was produced by wind rather than deposited by water.[63] On the sands are tracks of some twenty-seven different species of animals. These include lizard-like tracks, the tracks of spiders, and tracks similar to those made by present-day scorpions. The evidence from these tracks is particularly compelling. Studies on small vertebrates and invertebrates have shown that in wet or slightly moist sand, no trace of tracks is left. Only larger animals (the size of chuckwalla lizards) are able to make tracks in wet or crusted sand. Smaller animals such as millipedes and scorpions are able to make tracks only in dry, loose sand.

Think about this carefully. If the rocks of the Hermit Formation and other strata below the Coconino were deposited by an enormous flood sweeping the whole world, where did the survivors come from to wander about on the sands of the Coconino? Astonishing!

Surmounting the rim of the canyon, we struggle past the buff and gray layers of the Toroweap and Kaibab limestones. The upper extends beyond Flagstaff to the south, in the Painted Desert to the east and almost to Zion Canyon to the north. These strata record later stages of the Permian. The layers contain the same general types of organic and sandy materials commonly found on shallow sea bottoms. In places they are composed largely of the remains of marine life – shells, corals, and sponges. We can easily see the abundant, brownish, fossilized, coral growths interlacing the gray limestone itself. The coral growths are so abundant, the fossils so clearly oceanic, including occasional shark's teeth, that even to an untrained eye it is obvious that there were two successive times when the area was part of an oceanic incursion.

Is this the end of the sequence? Not at all. We might spend the night at a motel in the resort town of Tusayan just south of the Park. Close to and a little south of the town is a small, very red mountain, Red Butte (Fig. 1). On the south rim east of Desert View is its counterpart, a flat-topped mesa called Cedar Mountain. These mountains are made of sandstones and shales. Without doubt, they are the eroded remnants of a once continuous layer. The same rocks are found throughout southern Utah to the north, in the Painted Desert to the east and as far as Flagstaff to the south. Above the canyon rim they must have been stripped away by erosion leaving only the two fragments. These are rocks belong to the *Triassic* Period.

Triassic rocks are exposed in a long, diagonal line from near the middle of the northern border of Arizona to near the middle of the eastern border. Except for the two remnants above, these rocks are at a lower elevation than the rim of the canyon. Nevertheless, they are younger than the limestones at the canyon rim. How can we explain younger rocks at a lower elevation than older rocks? No difficulty here. The rocks found at the Canyon rim dip gently toward the southeast. These Triassic rocks are on top of them. As the Permian rocks drop down, the Triassic rocks on top of them drop down also. It would be more accurate to say that the Permian rocks, along with the formations making up the layers of the Grand Canyon below them, were at some time pushed up as a great rounded dome in a mountain-building process. At any rate, the Triassic rocks to the east and south of the canyon are unquestionably younger than the Kaibab Limestone at the canyon rim. The Petrified Forest of Arizona is in Triassic rocks. The splendid sets of dinosaur footprints in the Kayenta strata near Tuba City, Arizona, are in late Triassic rocks.

On top of the Triassic rocks to the east (still younger, it should be noted!) are *Jurassic* rocks. These consist of limestone, sandstone and shale formations. These rocks are continuous to the north, and form the magnificently shaped masses of Zion Canyon in Utah. As a matter of fact, they are readily followed north into Montana and southeast into New Mexico. A single formation within the Jurassic, the Morrison Formation, has produced skeletons of some gigantic American dinosaurs including *Brontosaurus, Diplodocus, Stegosaurus*, and *Allosaurus*. These kinds of dinosaurs are not found in any rocks below the Jurassic, and surely this is significant. The very earliest mammals are found in the Jurassic in other parts of the world.

Still further to the east, extending into New Mexico, north through Canada, south into Mexico, are rocks formed through an invasion of the sea. These rocks, belonging to the *Cretaceous Period*, lie on top of the Jurassic rocks and are, of course, still younger. They are filled with a great variety of marine fossils.

On top of these, still belonging to the Cretaceous, are rocks formed as the sea receded and left great accumulations of vegetable matter believed to have been formed in coastal swamps. This organic matter was buried by sediments brought down by streams, and so formed the coal beds on Black Mesa, Arizona, and near Gallup, New Mexico. Coal Mine Canyon is a colorful, spectacular, little-visited site between Tuba City and Oraibi, where there is a thin deposit of coal and also a bed of fossil oyster shells several feet thick. The top is Cretaceous rocks with the lower slopes formed by Jurassic rocks. It is a wonderful spot for a curious visitor to observe a fragment of changing earth history without having to take more than a few steps. These are oceanic deposits. In contrast to these deposits, nonmarine sediments of the Cretaceous carry fossils of the terrible *Tyrannosaurus rex*, the three-horned *Triceratops horridus*, and the enormous duck-billed dinosaur. (But these particular reptiles have not yet been found in Grand Canyon environs.)

Above and younger than all of these are the Wasatch rocks of Bryce Canyon, Cedar Breaks National Monument in Utah and the Chuska Mountains along the Arizona-New Mexico border. These rocks belong to the *Cenozoic* period. The Cenozoic includes the older Tertiary and the younger Quaternary periods. In the earlier part of the Quaternary the cutting of the Grand Canyon began.

In Cenozoic rocks are fossils of birds and fossil mammals: tiny insectivores to giant titanotheres. In these rocks no dinosaurs are to be found, no flying pterodactyls, no porpoise-like ichthyosaurs. This is strange indeed if all these animals perished at once in a universal deluge, but not strange if the rocks depict an actual historical sequence of living forms.

A major theme of many flood-geology writers is that no more than two or three geological systems in their "normal" order are represented in any one locality. Furthermore, it is vain to try to find many more, much less a complete series of all the periods. Such claims are, of course, totally wrong.

In the Grand Canyon and its environs there are *nine*, not two or three systems in proper sequence. How many would we expect to find if none were missing? Twelve fossil-bearing systems altogether. Note well, all these nine are in their "correct" order! In other parts of the world all twelve systems are found, all in their correct sequences. A list and description of these is outside our immediate concern.

What do these Grand Canyon sequences mean? If evolution occurred, this sequence is exactly what we would expect. If evolution did not occur but all life was created in a week of sequential, 24-hour days, how can this sequence of fossils be explained?

Most significantly, if all these fossil-bearing strata were formed in an enormous world-wide flood, how can one possibly account for obvious tracks of animals at several different levels, all supposedly formed after the first enormous waves of the flood had already swept over the entire earth?

Do the fossils and their tracks show that all forms of life have had a common ancestry? No. All they show is that the history of the earth included a sequence of living forms. This sequence can reasonably be explained by supposing a common ancestry. At least, the position of the fossils and fossil tracks are quite impossible to explain with the flood geology concept. Would the recreation theory explain the fossil sequence? That seems impossible. The progressive creation view would fit with the sequence of fossils in the Grand Canyon. The Grand

Canyon seems to leave us then with two choices. Either progressive creation, or derivation of all the fossils from a common ancestry. What other evidence is there?

Geographic Distribution of Life Forms

A question worth pondering is why there are no hummingbirds in Europe, Asia Africa, or Australia. There are 319 species of these tiny fliers, all limited to the Western Hemisphere. Most species are found in the tropics. If hummingbirds found refuge on Noah's ark, why did none of their progeny remain in the Old World? Is it possible that only one pair came through the flood, that pair migrated to the New World, and from that pair, in the few thousand years since the flood, all the various genera and species evolved? Or were the first pair of a number of species saved on the ark, but all those species divinely directed to migrate to North and South America and nowhere else? Why have they remained in the Americas? Do they lack the physical capacity to fly to Europe or Africa? If so, how did they manage to migrate to the Americas in the first place?

Possibly the strongest evidence for evolution emerges with a careful plotting of the geographic distribution of living animals and plants. The results seem to require one of two possible explanations. Either each species of animal and plant was created on the continent or island where it is now found, or a remarkable range of evolution has taken place.

How else can one explain the many families of animals unique to Australia, and the total absence in Australia of numerous other families widespread elsewhere on the globe? It is incredible to think that the Australian fauna migrated there from Asia Minor after the Noachian flood. If they did, why are there no remnants left along the migratory trail? Nothing remains elsewhere even remotely resembling the Tasmanian devils, the tiger cats, the wombats, the kangaroos, the marsupial moles, the koalas, the cassowaries, the emus and so many others. If our interpretation of the Bible requires that these creatures left the ark for Australia, one wonders how the sluggish wombats or the delicate koalas managed the trek.

One possibility is that God created all these unique species in Australia at the very beginning. Young-earth creationists can scarcely agree to that, however, for if the species were created in Australia, how did they escape annihilation by the Noachian flood?

The logical explanation is that the Australian subcontinent, once connected to the Asian land mass, was initially inhabited by various groups of ancestral organisms. Later, the connections with the Asian continent were broken, so that no migration took place from Australia to the Asian continent. Subsequently the species living in Australia gave rise to a great number of wholly distinct species. Meanwhile, animals in other parts of the world gave rise to species different from those in Australia. Groups that multiplied elsewhere in the world were unable to migrate to Australia, and Australian animals were unable to migrate elsewhere. As a result, the fauna of Australia came to differ markedly from the fauna of the Asian mainland. All this is described in numerous textbooks on evolution, and does not need to be detailed here. What is much less well known is that a similar phenomenon took place in the New World.

Flood geologists have made little effort to account for the distributional patterns of animals and plants. Their common explanation is simply that God provided the necessary land bridges and land rafts to ferry animals to otherwise unreachable islands and continents from the resting place of the ark. *Land bridges* are continuous extensions of land that may once have existed, but are now entirely submerged or represented by surviving islands. From the

Asian continent, for example, there seems to have been an uninterrupted avenue of dry land across the Bering Strait into North America.

Land rafts are common phenomenon. Along the margins of tropical rivers, vegetation grows out from the bank to form a shelf. The shelf is firmly held to the bank by a tangle of roots and vines. Then trees grow on the shelf, and when they die their trunks fall out into the river but are held in place by a continuous growth of vines, thus extending the shelf out still further. The process continues until the shelf becomes an extension of the forest, but a floating extension. On some of the world's large rivers, such as the Amazon, these shelves are known to extend out from the bank as far as one quarter mile. At flood times, sections of the shelf break off and float out to sea, carrying with them the animals that inhabited the shelf: lizards, snakes, birds, mammals, various invertebrates, trees, vines and shrubs. Such floating islands have been tracked at sea for over two years before breaking up. Scientists who study animal distribution credit land rafts for the introduction of many of the unusual populations found in remote oceanic islands.

Although it may be possible to credit land rafts and land bridges with migrations to the New World, there are difficulties great enough that nothing short of a nearly endless series of outright miracles can explain the distribution of many, many species from an ark located on or near present-day Mount Ararat to the New World. An example worth considering is the distribution of the mammalian order Edentata (also known as Xenarthra), an order which is limited in its distribution to the New World. It includes four families of animals: the armadillos (7 genera with 21 species), the tree sloths (2 extant genera of 1 species each and 12 extinct genera), the anteaters (3 extant genera with 4 species), and the ground sloths (many genera, all now extinct). The two-toed and the three-toed tree sloths are strictly adapted for locomotion in trees, coming down about once a week to urinate and defecate. On the ground they are almost helpless and walk with great difficulty.

Members of each of these families share a great many structural characters. These characters place them into a single natural order in the same way that shared unique characters place all rodents in a single order and all carnivores in a single order. The best explanation for the shared similarities is that each species in the order has had a common ancestry. Furthermore, it is reasonable to think it was in the New World they diverged from their common ancestor, since three fossil North American genera appear to represent a primitive edentate stock.[64]

How did all these different but related families get to the New World from the opening of the ark? A flood geologist might postulate an ancestral tree sloth migrating to South America on an oceanic land raft. Perhaps an ancestral pair of armadillos, an ancestral pair of anteaters, and an ancestral pair of ground sloths did the same. If so, it is marvelously coincidental that all came to the New World, left a fossil record in the New World, but in the Old World left no extant species and no fossils whatsoever. Furthermore, if an ancestor of each family did migrate to the New World, we are left with a truly remarkable degree of microevolution, for within each family are some exceptionally diverse members.

Young-earth creationist Kurt P. Wise explained such phenomena are the consequence of "similar organisms (fit for similar environments and with similar capabilities) traveling more or less together to similar environments."[65] It is difficult indeed to invoke this explanation for the varied families within the Edentata.

Other living mammalian *families* (not to mention many extinct families) that are totally limited to the New World include the anteaters, the pocket gophers (Geomyidae), the pouched mice (Heteromyiidae), the New World porcupines (Erethizontidae), chinchillas (Chinchillidae), nutrias (Capromyidae), guinea pigs (Caviidae), the capybara (Hydrochaeridae), agoutis and picas (Dasyproctidae), chinchilla rats (Abrocomidae), spiny rats (Echimyidae), mountain beavers (Aplodontidae), three other families of rodents, the New World pigs or peccaries (Tayassuidae), pronghorns (Antilocapridae), three families of New World monkeys and five families of bats.

Evolution of these species within the Americas provides a reasonable explanation for their distributions. There is simply no other explanation that even begins to account for all the unique species.

Seeming Impossibilities for either Fiat Creation or Evolution

At first glance some distributions seem incapable of explanation from either a young-earth creationist or an evolutionary standpoint, unless God created each species where it is now found. Members of the arthropod subphyllum Onychophora present just such a problem. What are these creatures?

When I was a freshman zoology student, our zoology class was asked to learn a great deal about one onychophoran named *Peripatus*. We were solemnly assured that it was a most important creature, for it was the evolutionary link connecting the myriads of arthropods with the segmented worms. (Our familiar garden earthworms are among the segmented worms.)

Modern evolutionists have quite reversed this opinion, at least if the late paleontologist Stephen Jay Gould is their spokesman. I recommend reading the charming account of onychophorans in his essay, "The Reversal of *Hallucigenia*" in *Eight Little Piggies*, even for those convinced Gould wrote nothing but lies.[66] In the entire subphyllum there are only 70 surviving species of these peculiar 2- to 6-inch long animals, which much resemble walking worms with short antennae. There are two families in the subphyllum. The family Peripatidae occurs in Central America, northern South America, West Africa and Borneo. The family Peripatopsidae occurs in southern Chile, South Africa, Australia, New Britain in Papua New Guinea, and New Guinea.

What is so remarkable about the onychophorans is that they could *not* have survived the flood without having been taken onto the Biblical ark. This is because they do not produce eggs that can be dispersed by the wind and they cannot stand desiccation, freezing or submersion in water. If they were on the ark they could not subsequently have migrated or been dispersed by sea transport to their present locales. Per Brinck pointed out that they only inhabit rotten logs, but the type of logs are so rotten they would break up if floated in the sea.[67]

On the other hand, how can their distribution be accounted for by evolution? Their evolution would require that some forebears managed to migrate to the distant islands and continents, a seeming impossibility. Those forebears would also seem to have been typical onychophorans, since both families are involved in a somewhat similar ocean-jumping distribution.

A not dissimilar problem, one over which evolutionists puzzled for years, is the distribution of species of the web-toed salamanders (*Hydromantes*). Each species of these small, delicate, long-tongued animals has a remarkably limited range. The Mount Lyell Salamander (*H. platycephalus*) is found above an elevation of 10,500 feet at the head of Lyell Canyon in Yosemite National Park, California. The Shasta Salamander (*H. shastae*) occurs in fissures and caves south of Mount Shasta in the headwaters of the Shasta Reservoir, California at 1,000 to 2,500 feet. The Limestone Salamander (*H. brunus*) is found in the lower part of the Merced River in California. It staggers one's faith to suppose that these or an ancestral species of *Hydromantes* could have migrated from Asia Minor following the Flood. Over a long period of time, and at a time when climatic conditions in California were quite different than today, quite probably before the uplift of the Sierra Nevada range, an ancestral species might have had a widespread California distribution. A process of limited evolution could account for the gradual adaptation of some residual populations to the localities they now occupy.

The problem with *Hydromantes* is that there are two other species, both in Europe! The Cave Salamander (*H. genei*) occurs in Sardinia, the Eastern Cave Salamander (*H. italicus*) occurs in a small section of Italy and France. Did God create them in Europe and create three different species in the western United States?

This is no different than the problem with the onychophorans. Both have a continent-hopping distribution that seems to pose as much difficulty for an evolutionary as for a flood geology explanation. With regard to the onychophorans, did God create each species or perhaps the first representative of each genus on the continents and islands where they are now found? This is not an unthinkable, but of course it would discount the possibility of a world-wide flood destroying every terrestrial animal except those saved on the ark.

These are not unique problems. There are numerous examples, which anyone can ferret out by going through world catalogs of various groups of extinct and living animals and plants. How can they possibly be accounted for either by evolution or migration from the ark?

Continental Drift and Its Consequences

Over a century ago geographers noticed that the eastern margin of South America, if pushed eastward, would fit nicely against the western margin of Africa, both in shape and in corresponding rock types. In 1912 the Austrian scientist Alfred Wegener suggested that all the continents at some long ago time were indeed fitted together to form one large continent. Subsequently the continent split into several pieces and the pieces began drifting apart. Wegener considered that they "ploughed" their way through the underlying rock propelled by the earth's centrifugal force.

His views were unacceptable to geologists because he could not explain why or how such movement would occur. If indeed at one time the continents were together, it is easy to account for the peculiar present distribution of species of the salamander genus *Hydromantes*. It can be supposed that at one time the genus was broadly distributed across one single continent, no doubt at a time when climatic conditions and the absence of certain types of predators favored its spread. Over millennia of time, the continents spread apart and climates changed. Predators probably also assisted the climate in the elimination of the salamanders in the intervening gaps, so that now there remain only scattered remnants of populations that once existed. A similar explanation could account for the distribution of the onychophorans.

At one time, according to this hypothesis, the continents were together as one large continent (Fig. 2). At such time the spread of an ancestral onychophoran to various areas would have been entirely possible. After the continents spread apart, their descendants evolved to become members of the various genera and species biologists recognize today.

Figure 2. How the Americas, now separated by the Atlantic Ocean from Europe and Africa, appeared during the Triassic Period 205-248 million years ago. The dotted line indicates the position of the equator with respect to the continents. (Redrawn from Berggren and Hollister, "Currents of Time," *Oceanus* 17: Winter, 1973-74.)

Continents drifting apart from a former common land mass would also explain many other strange distributional patterns. Salamanders belonging to the family Cryptobranchidae, "hellbenders" as they are commonly called, provide a fascinating illustration. One species (*Megalobatrachus japonicus*) is found in China and Japan. The only other living species (*Cryptobranchus alleganiensis*) occurs from Louisiana to Ohio and New York. It is difficult to explain widely removed populations of these animals. They are aquatic but fragile, and it is almost impossible to envision them surviving a flood of the magnitude required to form almost all of the sedimentary strata we know today. Migration through salt water would be fatal.

It seems we are left with but two choices. We can accept an evolutionary model coupled with drifting continents, or we can accept progressive creationism with some fundamental categories created when continents were still joined. A young-earth explanation, even if it proposes that continents were violently wrenched about in the flood, leaves so many unanswered problems one can only marvel. A reasonable explanation is that the salamanders descended from a common ancestral salamander and migrated over hundreds of thousands of years through fresh waters of the once, great, single continental mass to their present locales. The locales were subsequently separated as the continents drifted apart.

The question is, were the continents once joined? Or is the notion that they were joined a matter of wishful thinking on the part of evolutionists who desperately struggle to find explanations where none are available? Is continental drift a concept not subject to scientific falsification? Is it nothing more than a belief system? Or is it a fruitful scientific hypothesis?

There is little question but that it is the only possible explanation of the evidence, since it accounts for a multitude of phenomena far better than the theory of immovable continents. Also there are ways by which scientists could show it to be wrong, if indeed it is. One way would be to show that rock cores taken at regular intervals across the ocean bottoms, when analyzed for radiometric dates, all show the same age. Interestingly, analyses of the ocean bottoms have been made, but before describing what was found, and to understand the significance of what was found, we first need to look at a bit of fairly recent history.

The thought that continents are moving around, floating on currents of molten rock, may strike us as something straight out of 1920s H. G. Wells science fiction. It was, for that matter, a concept stoutly resisted by a number of eminent earth scientists well into the 1960s. Nonetheless, accumulating, corroborating hypotheses have elevated it into a theory as well attested, for example, as the theory that the Human Immunodeficiency Virus underlies the many sad cases of AIDS. Several groups of independent observations fell together to make continental drift an obvious conclusion.

Scientists studying volcanic flows noted that as lava cooled into rock, the minerals in the rocks were magnetized in line with the magnetic north pole of the earth. Experiments also showed that when certain minerals were melted and then cooled, their molecules would line up with the earth's magnetic pole. It was quite astonishing then to find that some older lava flows were magnetized in a line reversed by 180°, as if the magnetic pole of the earth had at one time switched from north to south. Still older flows demonstrated normal, non-reversed lines of magnetism. Yet flows even older than these were again reversed. Some of the pioneer work was carried out in Iceland, where long sequences of volcanic eruptions provided a clear picture of a succession of magnetic reversals. In fact, long sequences of volcanic flows, not only in Iceland but in other areas of the world with long histories of volcanism (Italy, Japan, Turkmenia and elsewhere) were found to exhibit similar patterns of magnetic reversals.

From these studies emerged the hypothesis that the earth's magnetic field has in fact reversed itself a number of times. In times past the needle of a magnetic compass would have pointed north, as it does today, but at other times would have pointed south! Why the magnetic pole of the earth should reverse itself is not clear, but it probably involves movements of melted material far beneath the earth's crust.[68] Whatever the explanation, it appears unmistakable that the magnetic pole has often changed from north to south and from south to north.

As these studies were going on, it was discovered that across the oceans the strength of the earth's magnetic field varies, and varies in a way not true of the continents. The strength of the earth's magnetism from place to place over the oceans can be measured by a magnetometer towed at the surface behind a ship. It can even be measured by a sensitive magnetometer carried by an airplane. The variable areas of magnetism across the Atlantic Ocean were the first to be extensively plotted. In the Atlantic there is an underwater ridge (mapped by the use of sonar devices), which runs for thousands of miles roughly half way between the continents, then terminates at the north in Iceland. One magnetic strength was found to extend in a line for thousands of miles parallel to the midoceanic ridge. Alternating with that line was another with a different magnetic strength. Parallel to that was a line identical to the first. And so continuing across the Atlantic were alternating lines of weak and strong magnetism, mostly trending north and south, some lines broader, some narrower. These lines are called magnetic anomalies, but the question is, what causes them? Why are they there?

Quite independently of any hypotheses about continental drift, investigators analyzed igneous rocks on the continents to see if dates could be put to the times when the earth's magnetism shifted. Particularly critical to the investigation, beginning in the early 1960s, was the development and use of an extremely sensitive mass spectrometer for potassium-argon dating. Slowly and painstakingly throughout the 1960s, as investigators collected and measured samples, a time scale began to emerge. The scale proved to be consistent, wherever applied. God in his great wisdom had left a record of the earth's history through magnetic reversals in the rocks. Wherever magnetized rocks were dated, the times of the reversals were the same.

Going back to the oceans, underwater ridges are known between other continents, just as in the mid Atlantic. In 1960, Harry H. Hess of Princeton University proposed that these ocean ridges are sites where upwelling basaltic rocks from the earth's interior forced the continents apart as the sea floor spread. Deep sea photographs and samples taken at the ridges showed without doubt that there are upwelling rocks along the crests. In 1963 Fred J. Vine and Drummond H. Matthews, and independently Lawrence W. Morley, advanced what was then a highly speculative hypothesis that the solid rock of the sea floor is imprinted with the record of field reversals in the form of a sequence of alternately magnetized stripes. They reasoned that if there are magnetic variations found at the surface of the ocean, these could be caused by adding or subtracting from the general magnetic field of the earth the magnetic effect of reversed and non-reversed rocks on the floor.

At the time, a majority of geophysicists, generally convinced of the fixity of the continents, were highly critical of the hypothesis. By 1968, however, the Vine-Matthews-Morley hypothesis was universally and enthusiastically accepted. Why? Studies of hundreds of cores taken from the ocean floors showed conclusively that the rocks did indeed have alternating patterns of magnetism.

What clinched the argument with finality, and drove even the most obstinate continental fixists to the position of continental drift, was this. The relative widths of the magnetic bands on the ocean floor correlate *exactly* with the time scale found for pole reversals in continental rocks. Placing the two scales together they form mirror images of each other. Why do they do so? The new rock wells up from the central ridges of the ocean at a steady rate. As it does, the rock becomes magnetically polarized and does not lose its polarization. When the earth's magnetic pole reverses, newer rock is imprinted with the reversed polarization as it continues to spread outward in both directions from the ridges. Still more rock continues to form, but when the magnetism of the poles again change, the magnetism of the newest rock also changes. Thus a pattern is created, a pattern that can be followed in cores taken from the floor and a pattern that can be observed at the surface (Fig. 3).

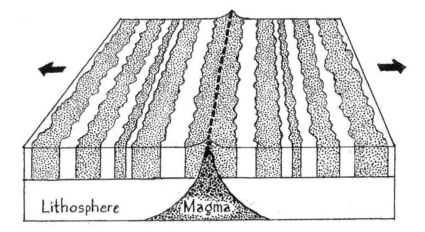

Figure 3. Sea floor spreading. Magma arises from deep in the earth along a central oceanic ridge. As it produces rock, the sea floor is pushed apart, and with it the continents. As rock is produced, it becomes imprinted with the magnetic polarity then existing. When the polarity changes, the rock is imprinted with the changed magnetic direction. Hence, there are bands of sea floor rock, some showing that it was made when a compass needle pointed south, some made when a compass needle pointed north.

Corroborating this remarkable story, numerous potassium-argon dates have been taken from ocean floor cores. These dates line up exactly with what was predicted. The youngest dates are at the midoceanic ridges, and become progressively older the further from the ridge the cores are taken. Numerous cores have been taken using the now famous deep sea drilling vessel, the Glomar Challenger, operated by the Scripps Institute of Oceanography of the University of California at San Diego. Some young-earth creationist writers have disputed the validity of sea floor spreading, but only by citing papers written *before* the present evidence was all in, particularly evidence from radiometric dating of the cores. Most people who are not geologists have little concept of the tremendous amount of data gathered by drilling into the ocean floor. Those who are interested, need to look up the 143 volumes (through May 1992) of the *Proceedings of the Ocean Drilling Program* produced under the auspices of the Joint Oceanographic Institutions for Deep Earth Sampling. Since the middle 1980s this story has really had no significant challenges.

It should be observed that the development of the theory of continental drift had nothing at all to do with efforts to support organic evolution. The supporting hypotheses were put together by geophysicists in an effort to explain some very interesting and puzzling phenomena. The holdouts among geologists, the continental fixists, were for the most part geologists brought up on the conventional interpretation of geological strata. Nevertheless, the discoveries were a boon for evolutionary theorists, because it enabled them to explain some very difficult problems in the distribution of plants and animals.

Some logical thinking

If we are forced by our interpretation of Genesis to believe that existing organisms migrated from the landing place of Noah's ark to the continents and islands where they are now found, we must be aware that we encounter truly insuperable problems. Solving the various problems by inventing a host of miraculous events which do not constitute science, and concerning which the Bible itself is altogether silent, is questionable at best.

On the other hand, if we can adopt a Biblical understanding of origins that allows for a great span of earth history with a sequence of life forms from simple to complex, from aquatic to terrestrial, then continental drift complements and enhances our view. The difficulty of accounting for distributional patterns is at an end. Such strange geographic distributions as those found in the onychophorans, the "hellbender" salamanders, the salamander genus *Hydromantes*, and many others can be satisfactorily explained by understanding that their migration between the Old World and the Americas was achieved when these continents were united.

The logic of the argument ought to be clear enough. Yet Christian anti-evolutionists have not been silent. They have sought to counter the evidence with arguments showing that the notion of evolution is biased and wrong. A few of their more commonly-repeated arguments will be considered in the following chapter.

CHAPTER 6

SOME OBJECTIONS TO THE DOCTRINE OF ORGANIC EVOLUTION

Readers are likely to exclaim, "But don't you believe the evidence presented by a number of scientists who are Christians and who have proved evolution to be absolutely false?" That is just what this chapter is about. How solid are the claims advanced by a number of anti-evolution popularizers? Are they speaking the truth? Are they misinformed?

I have no doubt regarding the sincerity and integrity of most Christian anti-evolutionary authors. Not for a moment do I question their genuine commitment to the Scriptures. I have many friends among them and value them for their faith in the Lord Jesus Christ. Nonetheless, the way they reason on the following issues convinces me of their faulty thinking.

Age Calculations from Radioactive Dating

Recent decades have witnessed the refinement and extensive use of what is claimed to be an accurate dating technique, a technique that involves the analysis of the decay of radioactive chemical elements in certain rocks. The dating of rocks by analyzing radioactive minerals has convinced geologists that the earth is old, much older than six to ten thousand years. It has also provided a convincing method for dating many fossil-bearing strata.

How do geologists date certain rocks by analysis of radioactive minerals they contain? Radioactive elements such as uranium-235 decay gradually into other elements.[69] An atom of uranium-235 decays into lead-207. In doing so it gives off seven atoms of helium.

Uranium-235 is one of several forms (isotopes) of uranium. An isotope of a chemical element is one made up of atoms with the same number of protons in the nucleus but with different numbers of neutrons. Uranium-238 is an isotope of uranium and decays to form lead-206.

There is no way of knowing when any particular atom of a radioactive element is going to decay. Nonetheless, in a gram of uranium-235 a certain number of atoms decay every year. The number that decays is always constant. Heating the uranium to the highest possible degree does not change the number; freezing does not change the number. Neither putting the uranium under great pressure nor in a vacuum changes the number. Hence, if one starts out with a gram of pure uranium-235, in 100 million years the amount of uranium will have diminished by a predictable amount and mixed in with it will be a predictable amount of lead-207. Each isotope decays at its own characteristic rate. Thus in 4,510 million years, one half the atoms of any given amount of uranium-238 will have decayed to lead-206. In 713 million years, half the atoms of a given amount of uranium-235 will have decayed to lead-207. A chemical analysis to determine how much lead is present in a piece of uranium will tell how long ago the uranium crystal formed.

Consider an example of how it works. First, some prehistoric animal (perhaps a dinosaur) dies and its carcass is washed into a lake where it is covered by sediments. The sediments continue to accumulate. The animal's flesh decays, but the bones remain. In time the sediments harden and become rock. The bones are infiltrated with minerals and become a fossil in the rock. Second, after a longer or shorter period of time, a column of volcanic rock pushes up through the sedimentary rock and flows over the top. In the column a chemical compound of uranium is incorporated in the structure of crystals which form as the rock cools. That is, the molecules of a uranium compound are distributed in the lattice work of the molecules of the crystals. Possibly other sediments will form and harden into rock on top of the layer of volcanic rock. Third, in the course of time the whole area is gradually pushed upward in a mountain-building process. Fourth and finally, erosion wears away some of the surrounding rock and exposes both the column of lava and the fossil. Eventually an enterprising paleontologist digs out the bones of the fossil and is most anxious to know how old they are. The answer in general is fairly simple: find a few of the tiny uranium-containing crystals and send them to an analytical chemist. From the amount of lead present compared to the amount of uranium, the date can be calculated. Now note that the date is not a date for the age of the fossil. The date is the date when the lava column formed. But since the column had to penetrate the fossil-bearing rock, the fossil must be at least as old as the lava column and perhaps a great deal older.

Young-earth creationists do not want to find fossils millions of years old, first, for that would deny what they believe Genesis 1 teaches. Second, it would provide evidence for evolution by providing the great span of time demanded by evolution. So they level the following complaints against this picture.

1. Such radiometric analyses represent not careful science but wishful thinking on the part of geologists. Young-earth creationists have often found citations of widely disparate dates obtained in radioactive analyses of the same strata. They claim the geologists pick and choose among dates and select those that best meet their preconceived views about the age of the rocks. It is true that early uranium decay analyses led to some quite contradictory dates. A dispassionate layman looking at many of the dates published in the past could only conclude that scientists better get their act together.

Nevertheless, as the technique was being developed scientists were not unaware of the problems. A major source of error results when lead is washed out of the sample before it is collected. If some of the lead is leached out, the date will appear much younger than it actually is. Some kinds of crystals are more susceptible to the loss of lead than others. When the uranium-lead method of dating is used, many samples have to be taken, the surrounding rocks analyzed for evidence of leaching, and other precautions taken. By exercising care, however, many dates have been found that are repeatedly confirmed and, most significantly, that are consistent with evidences of age measured by other methods.

With the explanation of uranium-lead radioactive dating given above, it nevertheless sounds as if the case is not terribly strong. Who knows whether lead might have been washed out of the crystals or uranium might have leaked out? Many kinds of crystals have their crystal structure broken down by the powerful radioactivity of uranium, thus allowing for the modification or loss of some of the critical materials. And for a truth, if the kind of dating described above were the only kind of radioactive dating available, the case would be much less than convincing.

Happily, it has been discovered that as certain kinds of crystals are formed, they will incorporate uranium but almost no lead. The familiar zircon is one such crystal. Radioactive decay can damage some kinds of crystals so that the lead can leach out. In zircon, the amount of uranium is small enough that the crystal structure is not disrupted and almost nothing is able to leach out. Chemical analysis of the uranium and lead in the crystal shows quite clearly the age at which the crystal was formed.[70]

This is not the place to get into a detailed exposition of how modern techniques of uranium-lead radioactive dating are carried out. It should be noted, however, that there are some quite precise ways of cross-checking the results to determine if any lead has been lost, and if so, how much. A person interested in pursuing this subject should look up a procedure known as the concordia plot, a procedure described in most geology texts and in standard encyclopedias.

It may be helpful to discuss potassium-argon dating as one confirming type of analysis. Uranium decays slowly, so it is most valuable for older rocks. Potassium-40 breaks down to the inert gas argon-40 at a more rapid rate. Half the atoms of any given amount change into argon-40 in 1,300 million years. The advantage of using the breakdown of potassium-40 for dating is that it is a common element. Being present in a great variety of rocks it makes many more rocks available for dating. Another advantage is that atmospheric argon is almost never incorporated in minerals as they are formed. Hence, if argon is found in a mineral containing potassium, it must have come from potassium decay. There are, however, problems. Barely over one percent of the potassium in a mineral is potassium-40, the balance being potassium-39 and potassium-41. Methods of analysis have to be remarkably precise to separate the isotopes of potassium and to make an analysis based on the very small amount present. Also atmospheric argon can contaminate a sample even as the analysis is being done.

A truly premier scientific accomplishment of the past century was the development of a precise and accurate way to do potassium-argon dating. The technique was developed through efforts of investigators working in a number of different laboratories in different countries. Their collective labors have made it possible to obtain consistent dates for specimens from the same collection of samples, even when the samples are worked up at different laboratories. The victory came with the development of an extremely sensitive mass spectrometer, one which effectively counts individual atoms in a sample being analyzed.[71]

In the earliest days of efforts to develop radioactive methods of dating, old rocks dated by uranium-lead methods might differ by as much as 20 percent, or even more. With current refinements, when rocks of an appropriate age are being dated, ones where both uranium dating and potassium-argon dating are applicable, the two methods provide essentially the same dates within the recognized statistical margin of error for each. So also do analyses of rocks using the decay of rubidium-87 into strontium-87 and samarium-147 into neodymium-143.[72]

2. Another complaint goes as follows. Perhaps ten thousand years ago uranium may have decayed at different rates than it does today. Who is to say that radioactive elements have always had the same decay rates or that there might not be some unknown factor in the past that has altered the rates? Perhaps cosmic rays, mysterious energy from outer space, were at one time so intense they drastically speeded the atomic deterioration of uranium, rubidium, potassium and other elements. Perhaps cosmic rays speeded up the decay so much that minerals appearing hundreds of million years old are really only thousands of years old.

What is involved if we suppose that a greatly increased level of cosmic radiation produced a change in the rate of decay? To my knowledge, this is the only possible cause proposed by young-earth creationists for a change in the rate of decay. What are cosmic rays? What they are before they hit the atmosphere of the earth is atomic nuclei traveling at speeds approaching that of light. They are known not to be rays at all, although they continue to be called cosmic rays. They come to the earth with incredible energy, but their origin is shrouded in mystery. Seemingly they are accelerated to great speed when they cross the shock front of a supernova (exploding star). When the "rays" strike the earth's atmosphere, they collide (fortunately for us) with various molecules in the atmosphere. This sets up a cascade of reactions, so that only remnants (particles formed from particles formed from particles) of the original atomic nuclei are seen. I say fortunately, because cosmic rays are ionizing. That is they change ordinarily unreactive molecules into electrically charged and very reactive forms. If we were exposed for a relatively short time to the force of cosmic rays in outer space, the rays would cause extensive damage to the chromosomes of our cells leading to the death of the cells or the production of malignant cells.

Suppose somehow a tremendous blast of cosmic rays reached the earth's surface. If powerful enough to get through the atmosphere and further to penetrate far enough below the surface of the earth to change subsurface molecules of uranium into lead, what would happen to life? It would be equivalent to living under a powerful, turned-on X-ray machine. Every living thing would be fried.

To counter the evidence calculated by geologists for the great date of sedimentary strata, young-earth creationists need a blast of cosmic rays coming shortly *after* the flood. This would give the strata their misleading appearance of great age. What would such a blast have done to Noah, his family and animals leaving the ark? Their deaths could not have been avoided.

3. A different kind of argument is that in the beginning God may simply have created mixtures of lead and uranium in the rocks. Thus some rocks with a large amount of lead in proportion to the amount of uranium would appear to be very old, but the appearance would be false. Henry Morris wrote,

> The probability is strong, however, that all these radiogenic
> "daughter" isotopes were either formed "in situ" with their

> "parents" at the time of creation, or else incorporated with them at the time of magma emplacement, so that the "apparent ages" were built into the radioactive minerals right from the time they were formed.[73]

Morris's proposal would be an instance of God creating rocks with a mere appearance of age. The only kind of answer a scientist can give to this argument is to remark that it is somewhat odd of God to create combinations of radioactive elements and their daughter elements in amounts proportionate to the positions of the strata in which they occur. In other words, God put uranium with more lead (old appearance) in a lower stratum and uranium with less lead (younger appearance) in a stratum above it, just the way geologists would expect to find it. Otherwise the argument has no answer from science. It seems to be a resort of those who want to use scientific evidence but find themselves trapped in a box canyon with the posse not far behind. Support for the argument must come from Scripture, and here the Bible does not respond with a happy smile. God is not a devious God; he does not make things appear differently than they are.

What must one conclude? Dating of radioactive minerals is a fruitful scientific enterprise. The Christian need not fear if geologists discover that the earth is very old and discover that fossils do indeed occur in a time sequence old enough to allow for evolution. What recourse does the conscientious Christian have? Not to deny science, but to look with a jaundiced eye at somewhat doubtful interpretations of Genesis.

Gaps in the fossil record

Gaps in the fossil record? That is one kind of compelling evidence cited by young-earth and progressive creationists to disallow the notion of evolution of life from a single common ancestor. By gaps, writers mean the absence of transitional fossil forms between many of the major groups of animals and plants. One stratum might contain an assemblage of fossil remains with each fossil species entirely similar from the bottom to the top. The stratum above may have a quite different set of animals and plants throughout. In most instances no rocks are found that contain fossil organisms intermediate between forms in the two strata, as might be expected if evolution took place. Interesting examples are common enough.

The water-inhabiting trilobites appear suddenly in the Cambrian period. They are arthropods, that is, they are animals with an exoskeleton, a segmented body, and jointed appendages just as the legs of crabs and grasshoppers but unlike any living arthropod. Nothing similar is known prior to the Cambrian.

Eurypterids, "water-scorpions," appear suddenly in the Ordovician Period. They also are arthropods, having an exoskeleton, a segmented body and jointed appendages, some species quite large, up to nine feet long. Most current invertebrate zoologists consider them a sister group to the arachnids (spiders, mites, true scorpions) and a little more distantly related to the king crabs. In other words, they did not evolve from the arachnids or the king crabs, just the reverse, if anything. Some biologists think they may be ancestral to true scorpions. Yet there has not been discovered a fossil that could be considered a conceivable ancestor to the eurypterids – they are just suddenly there.

The origin of flowering plants is a major problem freely admitted by paleontologists. There are no satisfactory links connecting them with possible plant ancestors. There are hypotheses of how flowering plants may have come into being, but no fossil evidence.

The flying dinosaurs, the Pterosauria, which include the bizarre forms so well-known to school children, *Pterodactylus* and

Pteranodon, appear in the Jurassic without any known connections to other thecodont reptiles. The same thing is true of the various groups of ornithischian dinosaurs, which include the familiar *Stegosaurus*, the crested duck-billed dinosaur *Lambeosaurus*, and others.[74]

It would not be at all difficult to list several hundred other groups of organisms for which there are no known intermediates connecting them with possible ancestors.[75] The champion polemicist for flood-geology, Duane T. Gish, has tallied a number of instances of gaps, in his opinion too numerous to be explained away by accidents of preservation.[76] Some of his examples are readily explainable, others represent challenging questions.

What are we to make of the gaps? On the face of the matter, it seems as if the gaps provide a solid argument against evolution, at least macroevolution. The evidence from the gaps seems compelling enough that both flood geologists and progressive creationists can insist that not all life could possibly have evolved from a single ancestor. Progressive creationists use the gaps to define the times when God brought new basic kinds into being. But are the gaps real or false appearances?

Until fairly recent years evolutionists persisted in Darwin's answer that the record was too imperfectly known. No longer is this a tenable response. Extensive geological investigations have demonstrated that gaps of a certain kind are really there. How do paleontologists, for whom fossils are but the frames in the evolutionary cinema of life, explain the gaps? Is there an explanation? Paleontologists have four primary answers why intermediate forms are lacking. A quick review of these answers will help us understand a basic scientific issue in the debate.

1. It seems obvious that numerous species that once lived have never been fossilized, or their fossil remains are so scanty it is unlikely

they will ever be found. The ancestors of a great many animals were soft-bodied and left no fossils. Soft-bodied organisms leave fossils only under extraordinary conditions. On the other hand, when shellfish, crabs, fish, porpoises and other oceanic animals die, their remains are consumed by scavengers and further reduced by chemical dissolution and breakage. Predators tear up and scavengers destroy what remains of terrestrial vertebrates. Rare events such as major storms that rapidly entrap and bury organisms appear to be required to incorporate most organisms into the sedimentary record. This accounts for the observation that fossils are often found buried in mass graves. Considering the circumstances required for fossilization, one would expect the rocks to contain only occasional samples of many organisms of the past.

2. Gaps are smaller in younger, more recent strata. This is a commonplace among paleontologists. It is exactly what one would expect, if the strata record great ages of time. The older a deposit the more likely it is to be worn away by erosion, warped and folded, or changed into metamorphic rock. This fact implies that many of the larger gaps may be accidents of geological change rather than genuine phenomena.

3. Many lineages come to resemble other lineages the further back they are followed in time. Hence many gaps are not real but are artifacts of our framework of classification. To select an instance, the modification of the horse over time is illustrated in almost every beginning college zoology textbook as a prime example of evolution. The smallest horse, *Hyracotherium* (more popularly known by the invalid name *Eohippus*) had four toes on each front and three on each rear leg. It had eyes relatively more forward in the skull than modern horses and teeth more adapted for browsing than grazing. Some species were only 18 inches long. If one were discovered running down

a street today, no one would take it for a horse. Yet between this small horse and modern horses there are transitional forms in which size is increased, the number of toes is reduced, teeth are adapted for grazing, and eyes are placed further back in the skull. Our modern horse, donkey and zebra have no more than one functional toe, the middle one, with the two adjacent toes reduced to small splints. Different young-earth and progressive creationists have recognized this but have pointed out that all of the forms, tiny *Hyracotherium* to the largest contemporary draft horse, are nonetheless horses. Why therefore should not one think that God specially created an original horse *kind* and all others came from this one ancestor?

Here is the rub. A similar sort of lineage connects the rhinoceroses and the tapirs and leads back to their small, ancestral forms. Titanotheres are now extinct, but at one time these giant ungulates roamed the American plains. They comprise another line of animals with graded ancestral forms, such as found in the horse, leading back to a small ancestor. What is altogether remarkable is that the earliest (most primitive) forms of horse, rhino and titanothere are all very much alike.[77] If these early forms were the only ones known to vertebrate paleontologists, they would be ridiculed for placing them in separate families. They are currently placed in separate families based on a classification of their *descendants*, not on the earliest representatives. There is no significant gap between the earliest known ancestors of the horse, the rhino and the titanotheres. This is one example among many of missing links that are not really missing.

4. There are gaps which are genuine gaps. These gaps separate biological species. Niles Eldredge, whose name some readers will recognize as one of the founders of the evolutionary school of punctuated equilibrium, has given us a wonderful example, fascinatingly summarized in a July 1980 article he wrote for *Natural*

History.[78] Eldredge is a student of the trilobites, an extinct class of arthropods that flourished in shallow seas from the Cambrian through the Permian. These organisms are special, since for the Devonian Period in Bolivia thousands of specimens have been collected and added to thousands of others from collecting sites in Brazil, South Africa, Australia and even Antarctica. The mass of material enabled Eldredge to follow fairly accurately the history of different species through time. Eldredge summarized his findings by noting that if evolution proceeds by small, slowly accumulating changes, he should have found evidence of it in the vast numbers of Bolivian fossil trilobites he studied. He should have found species gradually changing through time, with smoothly intermediate forms connecting descendant species to their ancestors.

Instead, he found most of the various kinds, including some unique and advanced ones, present in the earliest known fossil beds. It was obvious that species persisted for long periods of time without change. Unexpectedly, when they were replaced by similar, related (presumably descendant) species, he observed no gradual change in the older species. If he had observed gradual changes, they would have allowed him to predict the anatomical features of its younger relative, which he could not do. He went on to explain that the phenomenon of abrupt change found between species in the Devonian trilobites is similar to the picture emerging in other carefully studied fossil sequences. There are gaps found everywhere in the record separating one biological species from those that succeed it at a later date.

How do evolutionary biologists and geologists explain the gaps between individual species? There are two ways. One way is to suppose, along with Dr. Eldridge, that evolution is a bit jerky. New species are formed by jumps called macromutations (not the macromutations of special creationists). There are some genetic hypotheses to explain macromutations, but that is another story. Another possibility is to suppose that evolutionary changes are more gradual but occur in extremely localized habitats that are unlikely to be found by the most diligent paleontologist.

Are all the gaps explainable by the foregoing observations? That question possibly may never be answered. At any rate, the gaps do not provide incontrovertible evidence that evolution is false and that present day living forms could not have arisen from a common ancestor. It is at least possible that the conventional paleontological explanations for the gaps are valid. The explanations cannot be dismissed as impossible. We may desperately wish that the gaps would firmly give the lie to evolution, but if we are honest with the evidence and with ourselves we have to say that substantial objections to evolution must lie somewhere else.[79]

The Entropy Problem

Antievolutionists repeatedly shout that any program requiring evolution beyond each created *kind* is absolutely impossible, for it would require a decrease rather than an increase in entropy. What is entropy? What does it have to do with evolution? Whatever it is, various creationists probably cite it more frequently than they cite any other reason for denying the possibility of evolution. A dictionary definition follows:

> Entropy: A measure of the disorder of a closed thermodynamic system in terms of a constant multiple of the natural logarithm of the probability of the occurrence of a particular molecular arrangement of the system that by suitable choice of a constant reduces to the measure of unavailable energy.

Few of us find that wonderfully clarifying. If we read in creationist literature that the principle of entropy forbids evolution, and we look up the meaning of the word entropy, we might reasonably suppose that these apologists are on to something truly powerful. Instead of using the term entropy, sometimes the reader is referred to the just as mysterious second law of thermodynamics. Most take this law to be something only a highly trained scientist can understand, so when it is bandied about by Christians with prominently displayed doctoral degrees, the layperson believes that within their pronouncements truth must surely reside. On the contrary, the ideas behind entropy and the second law of thermodynamics are not difficult at all, however frightening these unfamiliar terms or their dictionary definitions.

Entropy is simply a way of talking about the loss of available energy. "Available" energy is energy that can do work. Let us suppose you have a brilliant idea for a perpetual motion machine. You have a heating coil that heats a boiler full of water. The steam from the boiler operates a steam engine. The steam engine turns an electric generator. The electric generator provides electricity to heat the coil . . . to heat the boiler . . . to run the steam engine . . . to turn the generator . . . to heat the coil . . . and so on. You do not want any cold air from the outside robbing heat from the boiler, so you put the whole contraption in a well-insulated room. Of course, you have to get the process started. So you bring in some wires from the outside to provide electricity to jump-start the device by heating the coil. The coil turns red hot. The water boils! The steam engine starts to chug away! The generator turns! You throw the switch to cut off electricity from the outside. Now you watch it run, day after day after day. But alas, no. In an hour or so the whole apparatus slows to a disappointing halt. What went wrong? Friction? That is the answer most people would give. Perhaps it played a minor part, but you smeared a very expensive and highly effective lubricant on every moving part, so the thing should have run for a number of months at least. Ignoring friction, something else happened. Part of the heat from the heating coil was lost to the air. Part of the heat from the boiler was lost to the air. Part of the heat from the steam engine was lost to the air. The air in the room got measurably warmer. Not nearly all the heat you started with was used to keep the cycle in operation. But cannot you somehow collect that lost heat and use it to heat water in the boiler? No. Whatever you do, in the long run the room will get warmer and your wondrous device will get colder. The energy is lost and you cannot get it back. Here is the point: the *loss* of that energy can be expressed as an *increase* in entropy. Engineers have a way of carefully measuring how much energy was lost, that is, how much the entropy increased, but measuring it is not now of interest. We only need know that it happens.

What is the second law of thermodynamics, so insistently hawked in creationist literature? It is a simple law. Of its own accord heat will flow from a hot object to a cold object. That tells why you lost heat to the air in your failed perpetual motion machine. The heat flowed not only from the heating coil to the boiler, but from the heating coil to the air. The heat flowed from the steam engine to the air, from the generator to the air.

How does this have anything to do with evolution by natural selection? To answer that question, we have to see *why* the second law of thermodynamics works.

I hang a pendulum inside a closed chamber. I use some device (possibly a thin metal rod that is inserted in a tight-fitting hole in the side of the chamber) to pull the pendulum to one side to get it started. The pendulum swings back and forth and continues swinging for several hours. Eventually it stops. Why did it stop? Friction (which we mostly ignored in our example above). The pendulum encounters molecules of air in the chamber. These molecules, as all molecules, are in constant motion. They strike one another in a very *random* way and bounce off to strike others. The hotter the temperature of the air, the more violent the movements of the molecules. They strike the pendulum from different directions. Just as many strike the pendulum from the right side as strike it from the left. The pendulum in its movement also strikes the molecules. Two effects follow. One, the pendulum is gradually slowed by the molecules hitting it. Secondly, the motion of the pendulum striking the molecules agitates them to a greater degree and the air in the chamber becomes warmer. The energy of the pendulum is decreased, the entropy of the chamber is increased.

Now if by chance, as the pendulum moves to the right all the molecules were to move to the right, then as it moves to the left all the molecules were to move to the left, and the molecules should continue moving right and left in concert with the pendulum, the pendulum would not slow down. It would simply keep swinging. What is the probability that all the molecules will move in concert? It is not inconceivable, but since their movements are random, the probability is impossibly small. That the random direction of the molecules is a matter of chance can be demonstrated by some statistical mathematics, but that is not necessary for our purposes. It is obvious that entropy comes down to statistics. Entropy increases because the statistical probability of all the molecules moving the same time in the same direction is virtually impossible.

Here is an illustration that will help us see this. We get ten students. They don't have to be bright students. They need be students adept only at catching things. We put the students in a circle. We give each of the five students on one side of the circle ten jacks, those small, six-pointed metal objects used in the game of jacks. The students are instructed to toss the jacks to others in the circle. They are to toss them to anyone they wish and those who catch them are to toss them in turn to anyone they wish. The game begins and is halted after fifteen minutes. What is the distribution of the jacks at the end of the game? They are going to be fairly evenly distributed around the circle. Most certainly there will not be ten apiece in the possession of five students on one side of the circle.

This game is another way of looking at entropy. At the beginning of the game the distribution of the jacks was *ordered*. They were all on one side of the circle. At the end of the game, the distribution of the jacks was *disordered*. The distribution was disordered because it is statistically improbable that all the players will decide to toss the jacks to the same student or set of students. They will toss them randomly about the circle. We can say from another standpoint that entropy is a measure of the disorder in a system. As the original order in the distribution of the jacks decreases, we can say that the entropy increases.

We can, if we wish, call the original distribution of the jacks, ten to each of five students on one side of the circle, an item of *information*. If I print on a piece of paper the sentence, "I love my wife," the fourteen combined letters and spaces make sense. The letters convey some information. If with scissors I cut each letter apart and toss them into the air, then try to read what they say after they fall, it is highly unlikely they will fall in an order that says anything intelligible. Simply by chance the information will have decreased, just as the order of the jacks in the circle decreased. Physicists talk about an increase in entropy both as an increase in loss of available energy and as an increase in loss of information. From this example, we can see why. In either instance an increase in entropy is an increase in the disorder of a system.

Here is where the concept of entropy bears on the notion of natural selection. The DNA in the sex cells of a male and female human or other organism combine in the fertilized egg and determine what the new individual is going to be like. The DNA consists of highly organized molecules that carry a great load of precise information. The DNA contains a code for every structure in the new individual. Supposing evolution to be true, the DNA (or RNA) molecules of the first form of life carried a very small amount of information, only enough information to code for a very simple protocell. As evolution progressed, producing increasingly more complex forms, the DNA had to carry increasingly greater amounts of information. But if this is the result of chance mutations, we should expect an *increasing loss* of information. The entropy of the DNA molecules should increase, not decrease. Or, to put it differently, the second law of thermodynamics says that a system depending on statistical probabilities will suffer a decrease, not an increase in information.

Many creationist writers contend that when one looks at the second law of thermodynamics one rings the death-knell for evolution. Any evolutionary advance through natural selection is simply forbidden. God created the first set of DNA molecules for each created *kind*. All the progeny of those created kinds, which may include a number of related species, possess the same DNA molecules, or else the molecules are in a form degraded by mutations. Because of the degrading effect of random mutations, their information content is less, not more. It cannot be otherwise.

How would some naturalist counter the argument that the second law of thermodynamics forbids true evolution? We are not here defending the godless philosophy of evolution by undirected natural selection. Nevertheless, if we are at all honest, we need to look at the issues fairly.

Either of two answers suffices to show that an antievolution argument based on the second law of thermodynamics is a leaky bucket. One is the question whether entropy applies to living forms in the first place; the second comes from an understanding of natural selection. The two answers are closely related.

The first answer goes back to our dictionary definition of entropy. It is "a measure of the disorder of a *closed* thermodynamic system." Entropy explains why our perpetual motion machine failed to work. It was in a tightly closed and insulated room. As the machine began to run, heat was lost to the air, the air became warmer, the entropy of the whole system increased. But remember that the device got a jump-start with electricity that was brought in from the outside to get the heating coil hot in the first place. Suppose we do not turn off the electricity to the heating coil. We let it continue to heat the coil. Obviously the contraption will keep going much longer. But you say, "We no longer have a closed system. Energy is being supplied from the outside." Exactly. And this is where the argument "entropy forbids evolution" breaks down. The earth is *not* a closed system. The sun supplies a continuing source of energy so that *with respect to the earth*, entropy is not increasing. Energy is available to allow biological processes not only to continue but to produce increases in complexity.

But is not the entropy of the entire universe increasing? That is an unanswered question. Even if it should be, it would not change the fact that for the lifetime of the sun the earth will continue to receive a source of energy from outside itself.

For the second answer, consider again our circle of ten students tossing jacks to one another. The original one-sided distribution of jacks inevitably becomes randomized. But what if the instructor of the students stands in the middle of the circle? As the jacks are tossed about he intercepts as many as possible and directs them back to one student. What will happen? That student will shortly accumulate all or almost all of the jacks and the distribution will become less randomized. Obvious enough. But where in nature is the instructor who is going to intercept the jacks?

The evolutionist has the answer. It is the environment! If, as organisms reproduce themselves over the centuries, there are random mutations changing the information of the DNA, of course the information of the DNA is going to get more random. But if a changing environment throws out all the useless mutations and retains those few that better fit the organism for a changed environment, the information content will increase. The environment is the instructor standing in the middle of the circle intercepting the jacks and redirecting them.

There is one situation, however, where the environment cannot play the role of an instructor standing in the middle of the circle. The origin of life is such a situation. To continue with the analogy, there is no point in having ten students standing in a circle tossing jacks until someone has persuaded ten students to give up their other activities and participate in the game. This is the problem of the origin of life: how in the first place to bring a set of amino acids or nucleotides together in such a way that they form a self-reproducing molecule.[80] This will require a *decrease* in entropy, and no one has shown how it can be achieved. The second law of thermodynamics, as Thaxton, Bradley, and Olsen have shown in *The Mystery of Life's Origin*, stands very much in the way.[81] A reader interested in the somewhat complicated specifics will need to consult this work.

The Christian, accepting the truth of Scripture, recognizes that there is another person standing in the middle of the circle redirecting the jacks. This person is capable not only of redirecting the jacks but of modifying the environment. This is God himself. His rôle will be considered in the following chapter.

CHAPTER 7

THE MYSTERY OF PROVIDENCE

On the preceding pages I defined providential creationism as the creation of living forms through a process of evolution guided in each step by God himself. What I did not explain is how providential creation, that is, the Biblical doctrine of providence, is to be understood. Neither did I develop reasons for believing this view to be true. It is easy enough to find fault with other creation theories. It is another matter to present convincing reasons why providential creation should be accepted.

Most evolutionists are convinced that the driving force behind evolution is nothing other than natural selection. Natural selection requires random mutations of the genes. Hundreds of experiments seem to have demonstrated that nothing but chance determines when and where a mutation occurs. Natural selection also requires a constantly changing environment. Physical factors in the environment are in constant flux. Biotic elements in the environment also shift in hundreds of unpredictable ways. These changes, although immediately contingent, can be traced back to points that have no assignable causes. The changes are random, unpredictable, uncontrolled. At least the best efforts of science have found no assignable control. The conclusion that naturalists inevitably draw is that life has been molded by nothing other than random events expressed in natural selection.

If all observable evidence points to random changes in the environment and random mutations, how then can any knowledgeable scientist opt for a theory of divine control? The course of evolution would appear to be just as unpredictable as its causes.

Problems for Natural Selection

In recent decades, a few biologists have taken exception to evolution through natural selection. For the most part their objections have received little attention and their reasons have not been convincing. In contrast, the 1996 book by Michael J. Behe, *Darwin's Black Box*, received unprecedented attention.[82] Much of the attention has come from antievolutionists, particularly young-earth creationists, who found in Behe a powerful champion. But they have misunderstood Behe. Behe did not necessarily argue against evolution. He argued against evolution by undirected, unplanned, goal-free, Darwinian natural selection.

Why does Behe, a biochemist, find natural selection unacceptable? Simply because there are so many structures in living cells that are unbelievably complex, each part depending on the full operation of other parts. It appears impossible for the structures to have developed through a gradual accumulation of many small mutations. He calls it irreducible complexity. Others who have taken up the cudgels have popularized the term intelligent design, which seems to be implied by irreducible complexity.

To make irreducible complexity understandable, Behe illustrates it by the familiar household mousetrap. The mousetrap consists of a wooden platform to which other parts are attached. There is a spring that brings down the hammer onto the mouse's body. Both spring and hammer are indispensable. The holding bar keeps the hammer cocked when the trap is set and also hooks into a catch. The catch in turn holds the bait. The catch is slightly raised, but is easily depressed when a hungry, unsuspecting mouse nibbles on the bait. When the catch is depressed, the holding bar is released, and the hammer instantly sends the hapless rodent to mouse Nirvana. The whole device is irreducibly complex in that no one part can be left out without rendering the mousetrap totally useless.

The mousetrap can be compared to any one of a number of complex structures in a living organism. According to the Darwinian paradigm, every complex structure arose from a very primitive structure. Mutations of the genes gradually added other parts or modifications. With each modification or addition, the structure had a useful function and provided the species with an increased advantage. In due course, the final complex structure came into being. Behe's argument is that a gradual accumulation of small mutations, such as Darwinian evolution requires, is impossible, since these structures would have been totally useless without every part in place from the beginning.

The Darwinian establishment – the great majority of biologists – has generally scorned Behe's work. It got a scathing review by Kenneth R. Miller in his book, *Finding Darwin's God* [83] Miller, a cell biologist and a professor at Brown University, is a classical macrotheistic creationist who allows nothing but natural selection to determine the course of evolution. Behe effectively (it seems to me) answered Miller in the printed proceedings of a conference sponsored by the Wethersfield Institute.[84]

Most of Behe's illustrations are easily understood. A few can baffle a reader who lacks a background that goes at least as far as organic chemistry. It may be helpful to see two examples (not from Behe) that are not dependent on a knowledge of biochemistry (although ultimately even the following examples trace back to biochemistry).

The sex life of the bed bug provides an example of irreducible complexity. To my knowledge no one has ever satisfactorily explained how this most unusual and interesting sexual mechanism could originate through a series of small, successively advantageous steps. There are four closely related families of true bugs (Hemiptera) that employ the same method of sperm transfer. The bed bug family, the Cimicidae, is the best known and most studied. There are a number of bed bug species, but the human bed bug (*Cimex lectularis*) is universally despised, for it lives by sucking blood from humans. During the day, the bugs hide in cracks of the bed frame and about the mattress. They pierce the skin and suck blood while their unwilling hosts are asleep. For reasons that will be obvious, their mating habit is termed *traumatic insemination.*

In the "higher" orders of insects, to which the bed bugs belong, the male reproductive organ consists of three lobes, which are outgrowths of the body wall of the ninth abdominal segment.[85] The lobes are made of chiton, a hard material similar to our fingernails. It is the same material making up an insect's outside skeleton. The middle of the three lobes is the penis (or more precisely, to use the entomological term, the aedeagus). The shape and size of the penis is quite variable in different insects, but in families of bugs other than the bed bugs and their three related families, it always has the same function. It houses the membranous ejaculatory duct, which conveys sperm into the vagina of the female. The lobes on either side of the penis (the lateral lobes or parameres) may be modified in any number of different and sometimes complex ways, but commonly are structured to lock the penis into the female ovipositor during the sex act. By locking it in, the sperm are deposited in the vagina where they are supposed to go. From the vagina the sperm go into a storage chamber (the spermatheca) where they are kept until released, one at a time, to fertilize eggs that are moving down from the ovaries.

If we assume that bed bugs evolved from a common insect stock along with other families of true bugs, we are faced with the problem of accounting for an evolutionary origin of traumatic insemination. In the male of all bed bug species, the penis is extremely reduced and does not transfer sperm to the female. The right lateral lobe is altogether wanting. The left lateral lobe is a curved, sword-shape structure. On one side it has a fairly deep groove which holds the duct that carries the sperm (Fig. 4). In the process of mating, the sperm are not placed in the vagina. Most astonishingly, the lateral lobe serves somewhat as a hypodermic syringe. It is used to pierce the abdominal wall of the female and inject the sperm into her abdominal cavity, not into the vagina. For the female this would surely seem to be traumatic!

Figure 4. The left lateral lobe (intromittent organ) of the male bed bug, which is used to pierce and inject sperm into the female abdomen.

In the human bed bug there is one particular place on the female abdomen where the piercing occurs. The right underside of the hind margin of the female fifth abdominal segment, and the front margin of the sixth abdominal segment, are somewhat curved to provide a guide for the lateral lobe as it pierces the thinner part of the abdominal wall between the segments. Inside the abdomen and lying above this point is an organ (the mesospermalege) into which the sperm enter (Fig. 5).

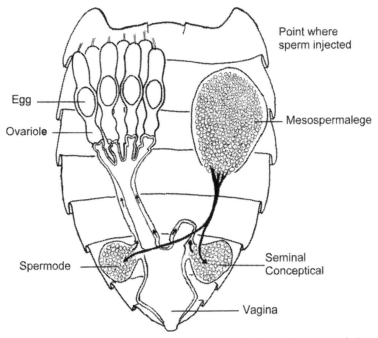

Figure 5. Internal reproductive structures in the abdomen of the female human bed bug. Black arrows show direction taken by sperm. The right ovarioles are not shown, neither are other organs found in the abdomen. (Redrawn from Carayon, 1966, somewhat simplified.)

The function of this organ is not entirely clear, but it appears to resorb the sperm plasma, probably to provide additional nutrients for the female. In the human bedbug there is a lobe at the posterior (rear) end of the mesospermelege through which the sperm leave to enter the blood cavity (the hemocoel) in the abdomen. (In insects the blood flows freely around the internal organs without being contained in blood vessels, although there is a heart that serves to keep the blood circulating.) This lobe more or less directs the sperm toward the seminal concepticals at the very back of the abdominal cavity. From the seminal concepticals the sperm enter tubular canals (spermodes) that lie around the two oviducts. Migrating forward through the tubular canals, the sperm finally reach the ovarioles, where the eggs develop. Here fertilization of the eggs takes place (Fig 5).

The human bed bug is more specialized than some species of bed bugs. In the bat bed bug (*Primicimex*), which ranges from Texas south to Guatemala, the piercing is not limited to one particular spot on the abdomen and there is no mesospermalege to intercept the sperm before they enter the blood sinus. Nevertheless, once in the blood cavity, the sperm follow the same route to fertilize the eggs.

Jacques Carayon, who has given us a detailed and fascinating description of this process, has only this to say about the evolutionary origin of traumatic insemination:

> Numerous indications, especially the accidental injection of sperm into the hemocoel among various Cimicoidea having normal insemination, lead one to believe that traumatic insemination very likely had its origin in individual aberrations of the sexual behavior of males. Unfortunately, it is impossible to explain why and how such aberrations, pathological in themselves and in their consequences, have become the rule in species and in entire groups.[86]

If, as the Darwinians claim, evolution takes place through the accumulation of unguided and successive small steps, it does seem impossible to explain.

One hypothesis is that at first the penis accidentally pierced the wall of the vagina, thus releasing sperm into the abdominal cavity. Even assuming this, how could injection of sperm into the vaginal wall in an ancestor be transferred to penetration of the *abdominal* wall? Did it start with another accident? It is difficult to imagine ancestral males jabbing randomly at a female, sometimes penetrating the vaginal wall, sometimes penetrating the abdomen, and achieving anything like an efficient process of insemination. From a standpoint of natural selection this would seem to be wholly unlikely, for it would be markedly less efficient than normal copulation.

But even if for some reason it was advantageous, how can transfer of the male sex organ from the penis to the lateral lobe be explained? The lateral lobe would need to be modified as a piercing organ and at the same time modified to carry the duct through which the sperm pass. Could this be accomplished with a single mutation? It seems unlikely, since the mutation would also need to provide a groove to hold the duct. Also essential to the whole system would be a modification of the musculature for the reproductive organ and its controlling nerve circuits. One or several mutations might modify the musculature and its nervous control, but without the modifications, efficiency would seem to reach a point producing negative selection pressures. After all, selection is presumed at each step to maximize reproductive fitness at the lowest possible energy cost. Because of this, it seems impossible to switch from the normal method of sperm transfer to traumatic transfer without several mutations, each of which would need to be simultaneous.

W. G. Eberhard cites J. E. Lloyd as supposing that traumatic insemination would have a selective advantage for certain males, since it would be a way of achieving sperm precedence.[87] They would get their sperm to the eggs first! This hypothesis might explain the selection of traumatic insemination in the first place, but not the steps leading to the modification of the male sexual organs.

This does not necessarily mean that traumatic insemination is not the product of evolution. If it is, it would seem to be a kind of evolution requiring guidance. That by chance all the necessary mutations could happen simultaneously, or nearly so, has a vanishingly small probability.

Another instance comes from one of the primary killer diseases in the world. The parasites responsible for malaria are one-celled protists belonging to the genus *Plasmodium*. They are injected into the bloodstream when a human is bitten by females of certain species of *Anopheles* mosquitoes. The needle-shaped parasites (at this stage termed sporozoites) are carried in the salivary juices, which the mosquito injects into the wound to keep the victim's blood from coagulating. (Follow the sequence in Fig. 6).

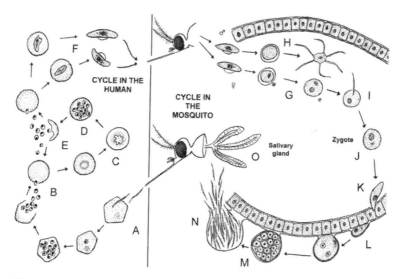

Figure 6. The life history of the malarial parasite.

Once in the bloodstream, the sporozoites are carried to the victim's liver, where they invade endothelial cells (cells lining small sinuses in the liver) (A). Here they multiply without sex to become merozoites. Incredibly, one sporozoite can produce as many as 20,000 merozoites in a single liver cell. After a short time they break out of the cells and enter the host's red blood corpuscles (B). In the corpuscles they transform into irregular, amoebalike organisms (trophozoites) (C). These divide to become other merozoites (D). Then the corpuscles rupture allowing the merozoites to enter other corpuscles and multiply again (E). This cycle is repeated a number of times until the victim's blood carries a large load of merozoites.

After a period, some of the merozoites in red blood corpuscles change into an amoebalike form prepared to become sex cells (F). (At this stage they are known as gametocytes.) Now they are ready to undergo a reduction in the number of their chromosomes. Every animal and plant cell, it might be noted, carries chromosomes in its nucleus. The genes of an organism are arranged on the chromosomes like beads on a string. Each species has a specific number of chromosomes. In different species the number may range anywhere from two to several hundreds. The malarial parasite, *Plasmodium falciparum*, has twenty-eight chromosomes in each body cell. (*Anopheles* mosquitos have six; humans have forty-six.) Some gametocytes are male and some are female. If the human host is bitten by another *Anopheles* mosquito, the gametocytes are sucked up with the blood and carried into the gut of the mosquito.

Sexual reproduction of the malarial parasite takes place in the stomach of the mosquito. In the mosquito the female gametocytes lose half their chromosomes (the process of meiosis) (G). So the lost half of the chromosomes are discarded. The remainder produce a female cell at this time with half the normal number of chromosomes, that is, fourteen. The male gametocytes go through the same process of halving the number of their chromosomes but end up as six to eight sperm cells (H). A sperm cell combines with a female cell (I) to make a new cell with the normal number of chromosomes. This is the zygote (J).

The zygote becomes a worm-like cell (K), which burrows through the mosquito's stomach wall. It forms a cyst (an oöcyst) on the outside of the wall beneath the membrane surrounding the stomach wall (L). A single mosquito may harbor from 50 to 500 oöcysts. The oöcyst divides (M) and gives rise to a number of needle-shaped sporozoites (N), thus completing the life cycle. Many of these sporozoites find their way into the salivary glands of the mosquito (O) ready to be injected with the next bite. Pity the poor mosquito. Needless to say, the cycle cannot take place without some damage to her. She must get as sick as her human victim – but not too sick to eat!

The great question is, how could this two-host life cycle have arisen through a series of small steps, each selected because it conferred some advantage over the previous form? The supposition that the ancestral parasite was limited to mosquitoes and secondarily came to be a human disease is not at all likely, for there seems to be no avenue through which the ancestral parasite could have spread from one mosquito to another. We assume the parasite had a history, so it must have been that the original host was a human (or some other vertebrate) and went through its complete life cycle, including its sexual reproductive stage, within a single host. Presumably some of the ancestral reproductive cells were ingested by mosquitoes and continued the reproductive process within the mosquito gut.

What is difficult to understand, if this scenario really happened, is how the fertilized cells (the zygotes) that were formed "knew" to bore through cells of the gut, not all the way through, but to encyst on its outer side beneath the membrane that surrounds the gut. Next, one or more mutations would have been required to modify the cells formed in the cyst into needle-shaped sporozoites enabling them to penetrate the salivary gland, and after injection into a human, to penetrate a liver cell. Without this mutation, or mutations, it seems the entire process would have come to an abrupt end.

Could it be that at the first, a mosquito simply picked up a few cells from a human (or some other vertebrate) and regurgitated them back into another host without a reproductive cycle in the mosquito? Such seems unlikely, since the mouthparts of a mosquito and the structure of its gut do not provide for any regurgitation back into the human.

Could it have been that just a few parasitic cells stuck to the mosquito mouthparts and were transmitted into another human host? That would have been an advantageous way for the *Plasmodium* to have spread. Then over time, the cycle evolved within the mosquito. This, however, would not account for the evolution of the sexual cycle within the mosquito, at least not without a number of simultaneous mutations.

Robert E. Snodgrass, a famous entomologist and an outspoken advocate of evolutionary naturalism, wondered how it becomes obligatory for some parasites to divide their developmental history between two different animals. His honest conclusion was, "...the known facts give us no answer."[88]

These are but two of many examples that can be described. The case for evolution by purposeless, unplanned, undirected, natural selection is fraught with problems never mentioned by the naturalistic evolutionists for all their claims to objectivity.

Did God create a great number of fundamental species in instant maturity with complex systems all in place? The evidence is decidedly against it. If organisms did not assume their present complexity by a process of unplanned, undirected, natural selection, what did bring about irreducible complexity?

The Providential Solution

In its simplest form, the doctrine of providence states that God controls all events in the universe in such a way that his goals are achieved. God, rather than chance or blind fate, is in control.

The concept of divine providence flows throughout the Bible.[89] Wherever we read of what God has done, such as his deliverance of the children of Israel from Egyptian bondage as recounted in Exodus and in Psalm 78, we read of providence. Providence is found in answers to prayer, as when Nehemiah prayed for Jerusalem and surprisingly King Artaxerxes was willing to send him to Jerusalem to rebuild the city (Nehemiah 1-2). Providence is seen in divine judgment for idolatry and debauchery, described particularly by the Old Testament prophets. It is how God acts in delivering those who trust and obey him and how he wreaks vengeance upon the wicked. It assuredly encompasses what he did in creation.

Occasionally providence is explicitly pictured as the unforseen and unexpected interaction of many seemingly unrelated events. The story of Joseph and his family in Genesis 37-47 is a familiar example. Joseph's brothers were jealous and hated him. His father sent him to inquire about the brothers' welfare as they tended sheep some distance from home. When he reached them, his brothers sold him to slave traders and led their father to believe he had been killed by a lion. The slavers sold him to Potiphar, a wealthy Egyptian. The calamity of being made a slave was mitigated when he was elevated to a position of responsibility and became the trusted manager of the Egyptian's estate. But this was followed by a second calamity when

Potiphar's wife falsely accused Joseph of attempted rape. He was thrown into prison, where he languished for several years. Eventually being released, he rose to a position of second in command to Pharaoh himself and was placed in charge of constructing great granaries in preparation for a coming famine.

A disastrous famine did strike the whole Near East. Joseph's position and huge supply of stored grain allowed him to save his father, brothers and their families, and to move them to the fertile fields in the Egyptian territory of Goshen. What appeared to be a series of defeating and tragic events turned out in the design of God as deliverance for his father, brothers and their families. In ways that could not be humanly foreseen, God was using different events to further his great purpose in fulfilling his covenant with Abraham, Isaac and Jacob to make of them a great nation.

The Christian should find no difficulty in applying the concept of providence to the entire world of living things. If in one of those interesting cycles of nature, a flood of Mormon crickets boils out of the mountain valleys of Utah and sweeping onto the plains devours everything in its path, it may be a calamity to farmers but it is neither unknown to God nor an event happening without his purposes. If a lynx pounces on a prairie dog before it can reach its hole, it is no tragedy. Rather it is part of the marvelously and incredibly complex working of God that preserves balance and order in the world. Is there a slight temperature rise in an isolated mountain valley? Is there a mutation better adapting progeny of some little millipede to that higher temperature? Both the rise in temperature and the mutation are the coming together of a design in which God is actively and directly involved. All such "natural" events, trivial and great, are part of the providential operations of God.

Science traces effects back to their natural causes and those causes back to prior causes. Scientists make a point of showing how causes and effects work the way they do through the operation of the laws of nature. Scientists see no need to invoke God as one of the causes. There are droughts that some years plague water-hungry California. The cause was unknown until recently. But meteorologists searching for some cause did not think of looking for a mysterious divine omen, perhaps a judgment on the excesses of Hollywood. Rather they looked for a natural cause and found it in "El Niño," a major warm water current of the Pacific that shifts from time to time. Similarly, so much of science involves working backwards, looking for causes and seeking to understand the material factors that direct the way those causes produce observed effects. If providence is real and involves the intervention of God in affairs of the world, and yet it is possible for science to trace one effect back to its natural causes, and those causes to other natural causes, and so on back, where and how does God come into the picture?

Some theologians have thought of providence as though God dips his finger into the natural order here and there to change the course of events. The universe presumably operates by laws which God established and which keep the universe on an even course. But affairs of the universe at times need shifting in response to human needs and circumstances. A number of thinkers have proposed that in some manner God adjusts or modifies one apparently insignificant cause to bring about an effect leading to a chain of other causes and effects. The final effect constitutes an unexpected or remarkable event. Meanwhile other events in nature keep on their expected tracks, being directed by natural laws.[90]

Such a view of providence is quite inadequate because it turns God into a bystander who is less than fully involved. God is viewed much as a child with a toy motorboat who sets its rudder and launches it into a small pool. Think of the rudder as the physical laws that keep the universe on course. The rudder keeps the boat going straight, but if the boat threatens to run into an obstacle, the child has to reach down and head it in another direction.

The God of the Bible is outside of, above, independent of the universe, and by his own choice is its creator. The Godhead existed before creation (John 17:5). Solomon in his inspired prayer stated, "Behold, heaven and the highest heaven cannot contain thee" (1 Kings 8:27). He is transcendent to the universe. The Psalmist declared (Psalm 145:3), "his greatness is unsearchable." At the same time God is totally involved in affairs of the world. He cannot be otherwise, for he is an *infinite* God. The Apostle Paul understood that he is "above all and through all and in all" (Ephesians 4:6). Psalm 113:4-9 expresses this truth in a delightful style.

> 4 The LORD is high above all nations;
> His glory is above the heavens.
> 5 Who is like the LORD our God,
> Who is enthroned on high,
> 6 Who humbles Himself to behold
> *The things that are* in heaven and in the earth?
> 7 He raises the poor from the dust,
> And lifts the needy from the ash heap,
> 8 To make *them* sit with princes,
> With the princes of His people.
> 9 He makes the barren woman abide in the house
> As a joyful mother of children.
> Praise the LORD!

Verses 4-6 picture his exalted station far above the earth and the heavens. Then verses 7-9 speak of his involvement in the affairs of humankind. A correct view of providence recognizes this teaching of Scripture. As an infinite God, his omnipresence is far more than merely "being around" in the universe making occasional adjustments to keep things on course. He is somehow present in every atom of the universe. If he is infinite, the furthest flung galaxy down to every incredibly minute subatomic particle are all in his hands.

Furthermore, God's power has no limits or bounds. God's own declaration to Abraham in Genesis 17:1 was, "I am God Almighty." Romans 4:17 is one of many passages teaching that God can and has done the absolutely unimaginable. He is the One "who gives life to the dead and calls into existence the things that do not exist."

God need not stick his finger in now and then to effect changes he wants. Every particle of the universe moves and functions *as if* it were his body. It is not his body. God is not identical with the universe. An analogy is that of a master pianist whose fingers range over the entire keyboard to produce the most melodic, rhythmic and harmonious sounds, as if the piano were a very part of him. Every subatomic particle in the universe is a piano key for the infinite God. The universe is his grand melody. The melody includes dissonance where it fits the Composer's purposes. Taken by itself a discordant sound is disconcerting, but in a succession of chords it leads to a richer composition. Every aspect of the universe, including calamitous and seemingly untoward events, is fulfilling God's purposes. This seems to be no less than what is required by the revelation granted us in the Bible.

How can irreducible complexity arise? It need not be by an instantaneous creative act. Complexity of any degree is no problem for a God who controls the movement of every subatomic particle. He can arrange two, three, four, five or six simultaneous mutations as his design dictates. He is, in fact, responsible for every mutation and for every slight modification of the environment, so that every step in the evolutionary sequence is his personal choice. It is reasonable for the Christian, therefore, to term irreducible complexity "intelligent design." The designer is the God of the Bible.

It is entirely possible that God did not use, or seldom used, simultaneous mutations to bring about complex structures. We can never know just what he did. So much we don't know because fossil preservation captures only fragments of ancient life. God may often have used intermediate byways which no biologist has yet imagined. God may have first directed the change of the male bed bug sex organ from penis to lateral lobe for an entirely different purpose than traumatic insemination. (Biologists term this preadaptation.) But the modifications were all arranged by God.

For the Christian who accepts the Biblical description of an absolutely supreme and infinite God, there is no alternative. By his will and by his power every necessary mutation, and every essential environmental change took place. Scientists examining the surface appearance see natural selection. Should scientists continue investigating problems that seem to fall under the rubric of irreducible complexity? Absolutely! But whatever they may find, *natural selection is no more than surface appearance.* It is not what goes on underneath and out of sight.

It should be evident, but it needs reaffirmation, that the doctrine of providence is not based on any scientific observation. It is a faith-based truth, faith in teaching of God's Word. No less, of course, is naturalism faith-based, for the conviction of many scientists that God could not be present directing natural selection does not come from experimentation and observation! (The observations of Darwin and others that animal suffering, including human suffering, is unworthy of God will be considered below.)

Yet if divine direction is responsible for all that has come to pass, how do we answer the objection that chance appears to reign supreme? It is difficult to deny chance when we repeatedly roll a die and note that it is impossible to predict which number will come up. Does God actually determine the outcome? If we are at a gaming table in Las Vegas, does God decide whether we win or lose?

Chance and Providence

To all appearances, everything in nature is governed by chance. If we assign ten people each the task of flipping two coins a hundred times so that we have 1,000 results, we can confidently predict that both coins will come up heads very close to 250 times, both tails very close to 250 times, and one head and one tail very close to 500 times. The more times the coins are flipped, the closer we will come to a 1:1:2 ratio, but we never know which way a coin will land on any particular toss. If we cross a hundred pink flowered snapdragons with a hundred other pink flowered snapdragons, we can be quite sure that the plant's reproductive mechanism will function randomly just as did the coins. We plant the thousands of seeds produced and when they mature we find one quarter of the plants with red flowers, one quarter with white flowers, and one half with pink flowers. The same 1:1:2 ratio obtains, although there is no possible way of predicting which cross will produce a red, a white or a pink flowered plant. It appears to be nothing but chance. Is God absent from such occurrences? Does God stand off and let the world run by random events? It seems so.

Naturalistic biologists have no doubt but that genuine randomness ultimately controls all of nature. Atoms and molecules in chemical reactions obey laws of probability, whether they are non-living reactions or reactions within a living being. In plants and animals the segregation of chromosomes at meiosis (to make sex cells with half the normal number of chromosomes) operates through probability, something which accounts for Mendelian laws of genetics. Background radiation affects chromosomes in a wholly random way, leading to unexpected mutations. This is what science observes. In fact, it is *the only thing* science observes. If there is some other controlling force, science has never been able to detect it.

What ought to be obvious is that the *appearance* of chance is no less than what would be expected with God in complete control. This is not our ordinary way of thinking about God. Yet a bit of reflection shows it is necessary.

Anyone who has had high school Biology and has looked through a microscope at a drop of water from a hay infusion is acquainted with Brownian motion. A tiny live bacterium is seen incessantly bouncing back and forth. The bacterium has no way to move on its own. Furthermore, the motion seems quite random. Why this movement? It is caused by a continual bombardment of the bacterium by molecules of water, which themselves are in motion. The erratic and seemingly chancy movement of the bacterium is visible evidence, even if secondhand, of the constant movement of molecules in the water in which it lives. The direction of any one molecule is, of course, contingent on how it is bounced off other molecules and how they in turn are being bounced off still other molecules. Nevertheless, there is enough play in the motion of the molecules that chance seems an inevitable component of the motion. Is it not possible to think that God would maintain just this kind of molecular movement and that there is no chance? The movement of molecules is a type of regularity absolutely essential for thousands of kinds of chemical reactions including those within every living being. The bouncing bacterium could not carry out functions of respiration and ingestion of nutrients without being in an environment of constantly changing molecules. Is

God in personal control of each incredibly minute molecule? Yes, since he is the *infinite* God of the Bible. There is neither microscopic nor macroscopic limit to his reach.

If God directs atoms and molecules in paths that are necessary for the function of chemical and physical actions, over what parts does he exercise control? The answer is that *everything* is under his control. He does not control a few key elements with the effects filtering down to the billions of uncontrolled elements. If, as a master pianist, God has *all* the atoms of the universe as his keyboard, he can play some sustaining notes on an enormous number of keys, while striking different notes or succession of notes with other keys. We need to think of God as a pianist with more fingers than there are subatomic particles in the universe, for our God is an infinite God. If he is infinite, he surely has the capacity to be in total control.

God need but direct the decay of a single radioactive atom at a particular second of time to make sure some selected atom or molecule is in the path of its emitted gamma ray. That would produce the effect he wants, yet all the while keeping other atoms and molecules in their expected (normal) paths. The effects of the decay, although directed toward a specific outcome, could never be detected by statistical analysis. This is not God putting his hand in here and there, since even the selected molecule in the path of the gamma ray would be at precisely the right place at the time of the ray's arrival. A chemical reaction between two atoms that rarely combine could be achieved for a specific purpose by a slight alteration of the usual orbit of an electron. The formation of the molecule could have an apparent chain effect of great significance, yet no physical analysis would see the working of God in it. This is nothing less than what would be expected from an infinite God, since every least subatomic particle is constantly in the course of his choosing.[91]

How can God exercise control over a single atom or subatomic particle? What mechanism might he employ? It cannot be that God is somehow identical with the particle, as pantheistic and panentheistic theologians and philosophers suppose. That notion would identify the processes of the world with the inner Trinitarian life of God. The God of the Bible is transcendent to the world and is its creator. The puzzle is how a non-material God can exercise control over material stuff. The answer, of course, is totally beyond us, for we do not even know what matter is. What is a quark, a lepton, a gluon, these ultimate divisions that make up the more familiar subatomic particles? They can be described mathematically and their paths can be studied when they collide in a cyclotron, but that does not tell us what they are. God's ways are even more inscrutable, so the question has no available answer.

Just because randomness appears everywhere in nature, and because science can discover no pattern that cannot be attributed to chance, does not mean that God is not working throughout nature. The randomness is a superficial appearance which in no way prohibits providential control by an infinite God. One who thinks the surface appearance of things removes God from the picture has not drawn the conclusion from science, but has made a metaphysical judgment.

What I have just described, of course, is also a metaphysical judgment. It is, however, a judgment based on my confidence that the God described in the Bible, the God of infinite power, is the God of reality.

Miracles and Natural Law

All natural science operates on the supposition that natural phenomena are governed by laws. The supposition stands implicitly behind every discovery in science. The supposition is, as philosopher of science Aharon Kantorovitch stated, "the most fundamental *metaphysical* belief behind natural science."[92] (Italics mine.) There are no experimental data to prove the belief. Yet it has held up remarkably well.

How can the laws of nature be real laws, if in providence God is able to modify events within nature? The answer is that God is in control of all events, so that what we perceive as laws are not independent of him but instead are the *regularities that he continually maintains*. Science discovered the laws, which have the appearance of independent entities. Yet they are not. God did not create laws as powers separate from himself. On the contrary, through Christ he is "upholding (or sustaining) the universe by the word of his power" (Hebrews 1:3). The laws are expressions of his moment by moment will. The universe maintains its law-like regularity with atoms behaving as we think atoms are supposed to behave and molecules vibrating and moving as they do because God maintains them in just this way. The probabilities that follow such things as repeated tosses of a coin also constitute regularities maintained by God. If 1,000 coin tosses yesterday resulted in 990 heads and ten tails, but today in ten heads and 990 tails, the universe would be irrational. An erratic universe could not be a universe under the direction of a God whose "faithfulness endures to all generations." Each fall of a tossed coin can be analyzed as a contingent event. At the same time, present in every fall is the controlling although invisible hand of God.

If God's purposes require it, he is not bound to maintain atoms and molecules in our concept of law-like order. A miracle is not God violating the laws of nature, neither is it God invoking some law of which we are unaware, since what appear to be laws independent of God are no more than *appearances* of his sustaining and regulating power. A miracle is God maintaining the universe in a way that meets the needs of his providential design. This does not mean the universe is irrational, but in a miraculous event such as the resurrection of Christ, there is a level of rationality beyond what can be analyzed by humans.

Does God control the regular randomness of a roulette wheel at an Indian gaming casino? Absolutely. It is part of his maintenance of law-like order. If you pray earnestly for a million dollars before slipping a dollar coin into a slot machine, will God answer that prayer? Don't blame God if you lose the buck, and a hundred or so that follow. After all, the slots are set for much less than an even chance of giving you your money back. God keeps his universe on track, even in maintaining regularities for the profit of Indian tribes.

Can God produce a big win? Of course. Why doesn't he, when you are sure you deserve a big win. After all, you are a true believer, you don't cheat on your spouse, and you haven't missed church for almost a year. Romans 8:28 has the answer. "We know that in everything God works for good with those who love him, who are called according to his purpose." For your own good, God knows that you need the discipline of losing!

Suffering and Providence

Suffering figures largely in arguments relating to creation. Many young earth creationists contend that before man's appearance on the first week of creation there could have been no animal life with its attendant predators and disease over the millennia, for that demands suffering. Yet Biblically, they say, suffering is impossible before man's fall into sin. Naturalists, on the other hand, argue that the existence of suffering negates the concept of God, at least the concept of a benificent God who has a hand in creation and in human affairs.

A famous quotation from a letter by Charles Darwin to the American botanist Asa Gray well illustrates the problem: "I cannot persuade myself that a beneficent & omnipotent God would have designedly created the Ichneumonidae with the express intention of their feeding within the living bodies of caterpillars, or that a cat should play with mice."[93]

If God exists and is responsible for every mutation, Christians are confronted with seemingly an even more intractable problem. How can we balance an equation in which a benevolent and all-powerful God is on one side and horrible, human, genetic malformations are on the other? Tay-Sachs disease, for example, is a disorder resulting from a mutation of a gene. Child victims of the disorder develop loss of motor coordination, blindness and insanity. Typically they die by the age of four. Except for genes carried on the male X chromosome (one of the sex chromosomes), genes occur in pairs. One pair of chromosomes carries the two genes that, when each is recessive, are responsible for Tay-Sachs. Being recessive, the mutated gene is not expressed when the corresponding gene is normal. When a single mutated gene is carried as a recessive by each of two otherwise normal parents, one fourth of their children can be expected to have Tay-Sachs, because one fourth of their children will likely inherit the mutation in both corresponding chromosomes. Because the disorder can be tracked through family trees, and because the ratio of affected children can be predicted statistically, it appears that random chance, not God, is responsible.

There are hundreds of other genetic diseases resulting from the inheritance of a mutated gene. Some genetic diseases are invariably lethal (that is, resulting in death before the reproductive age), some are badly crippling, some result in no more than inconvenient defects. Red-green color blindness is an example of an inconvenient inherited defect. So is the ordinary inheritance of six fingers or six toes (more common than most people realize).

Edward O. Wilson, a disbelieving Harvard biologist famous both for his investigations on social insects and for his theoretic evolutionary studies, insists that God did not plan or direct the creation of life. In *The Diversity of Life* he explains the presence in humans of the gene for sickle cell anemia.[94] The gene is found in areas of tropical Africa, the eastern Mediterranean, the Arabian Peninsula and India, where mosquitoes carry the parasite for the commonly fatal *falciparum* malaria. In cells of the human body, two corresponding chromosomes each carry the gene responsible for the production of hemoglobin in the red blood corpuscles. The body uses hemoglobin to transport oxygen from the lungs to all the tissues of the body. There are two alternate forms of the gene for hemoglobin. Most individuals have two identical genes for normal hemoglobin. Each of the two is on a corresponding member of a pair of chromosomes.

If instead of two normal genes, a person has one gene that codes for sickle cell anemia and one that codes for normal hemoglobin, the individual is happily resistant to *falciparum* malaria and experiences only the most minor anemic effects. If however, an individual has two genes for sickle cell anemia, the individual is resistant to malaria, but dies painfully, usually before reaching maturity. This is because some of the blood corpuscles have a sickle-shape, which blocks the capillaries and impedes the flow of blood. As with all genes except those carried on the sex chromosomes, each child receives one from the mother and one from the father. If the mother and father each have one gene for normal hemoglobin and one for the kind that causes sickle cell anemia, it appears to be a matter of chance which genes the child receives. Since such chance determines how the chromosomes segregate in forming sex cells, and which cells combine to produce a fertilized egg, a child may have both genes normal, a one-quarter probability, both genes defective, a one-quarter probability, or one normal and one defective, a one-half probability. It is the same ratios that comes from flipping two coins a number of times and counting how many come up both heads, how many both tails, and how many one head and one tail.

Where did the defective hemoglobin gene come from? At some point in human history one of the normal genes changed. A mutation produced a glitch in the DNA code. The alteration permitted the substitution of one amino acid (valine) for the normal amino acid (glutamic acid) at two positions in the strings of 574 amino acids making up the hemoglobin molecule. This mutation has been perpetuated, because it confers a survival and reproductive advantage for people carrying it and living in malaria-infested areas. Those who have it lose only one-quarter of their children to anemia and one-quarter to malaria. Those without it lose almost all their children to malaria.

Wilson wrote, "The sickle-cell trait puts a twist on moral reasoning that is worth a moment's reflection." He explains that the frequency of the gene in human populations is rather closely correlated with the frequency of the malarial parasite. It is there because of the "mindless" evolutionary process of natural selection. Those who die of malaria do so because they are in a hostile environment. Those who die of a double dose of the sickle gene are "Darwinian wreckage, cast off as the accidental side product of a chance mutation." Unfortunates in these tropics die in tragically large numbers because in this instance natural selection is balanced. That is, the population is not completely wiped out, nor has a mutation occurred that would give total immunity against the fatal effects of the disease.

The conclusion Wilson reaches on pages 79-80, is that nothing more than undirected, unplanned natural selection governs what we are, what genes we possess, what controls our destinies. "No gods decreed it, no moral precept emerges from it." Natural selection is the creator.

If there is a God, how can he be so seemingly indifferent to the fact that individuals with both alleles for the sickle cell gene do not live much past twenty, if that long, and people in malaria-infested regions who carry both alleles for normal blood corpuscles die willy-nilly from a terrible, mosquito-borne disease? Whether there is an answer that will satisfy Wilson or not, Wilson has not considered the possibility that there are purposes of God wholly outside his ken. Wilson is making a value judgment based on human knowledge, and in doing so he is exercising faith. He believes that his judgments of how God ought to act, should God exist, are sufficient to negate the possibility of his hand in nature.

Since God controls every mutation event, is God indifferent to the effects of mutations? Someone with a Biblically-informed faith must answer, of course not! In every circumstance God has a purpose. Each purpose is tooled to God's need to deal with willful human autonomy and selfish actions. His purpose is to lead humans to dependence upon his grace. Can I or anyone see how God is using genetic ratios to accomplish his purposes? No, for our finite minds cannot look into his infinite mind.

The Christian answer considers the fact that God has total knowledge of every freely chosen thought and deed of every human. God knows the thoughts of the victims of sickle cell anemia. God knows the thoughts of parents who see their children suffer. God deals with natives of malaria-infested countries as well as with the rest of us ,in both mercy and justice. Suffering of any kind may and ought to drive one to him for mercy. When it does, his love triumphs. When anyone remains obdurate, cherishing wickedness and trusting in empty idols, divine justice necessarily takes over. Knowing the detailed thoughts of every human, God makes no mistakes, even if our statistical analyses seem to say he isn't around.

This is an issue that needs to strike the conscience of every Christian. The Christian needs to be exercised with love for these unfortunate victims of malaria and sickle cell anemia. They are eternal souls for whom Christ also came and suffered at Calvary. Compassion to relieve their suffering, and the message of eternal life to deliver their souls from futility, is a solemn Christian responsibility.

From the Christian standpoint the answer to Wilson consists in this: life for the believer is not exhausted by the death of the physical body. There is an "eternal weight of glory" awaiting those willing to accept God's gracious provision of forgiveness and justification. The Christian responsibility is to see that no one is lacking an opportunity to observe the love of God through our love, and to hear and believe the truth. There is suffering for all mankind, suffering that results directly and indirectly from sin. Given this, God would indeed be immoral if this present suffering were in truth the end of life. But God has made a provision whereby this present suffering is only the vestibule to an eternity of joy for those willing to trust the Messiah of Calvary. Furthermore, God grants mercy to endure suffering in answer to the prayer of faith, and even to experience gracious relief.

Wilson's anti-theistic objections have a convincing ring, for they are based on modern population genetics. Nevertheless, his style of objection has a long history, for atheists have always been quick to seize on human suffering to deny the existence of a loving God. Theists rightly counter that without a personal God, there are no solid grounds for human moral judgments. Without God, right is whatever capricious societies determine it to be, plus what serves one's convenience. Given no God, the subjugation of women by Muslim societies is not wrong in principle. Terrorist murders are not morally wrong except in the judgment of the victim nations. Apart from an absolute standard of morality, there is no ground to condemn a child sex-abuser except when a society judges it to be wrong. Not all societies consider it wrong. Without a righteous God there are no absolutes, and Wilson has no basis for his complaint about human suffering.[95]

Providence and Human Freedom

If the omnipotent God controls every least movement of every subatomic particle, how do humans have any freedom? Does not this mean that even our innermost thoughts are determined by God, that we are essentially puppets of a controlling Sovereign?

To many this seems an inescapable conclusion. The Bible speaks of God as having all knowledge, including a knowledge of the future. If God knew before creation how everything would come about, how are events not predetermined? He could not know, it seems, unless he in fact predetermined them. Theologians who are followers of the devout Genevan reformist John Calvin connect providence with strict predestination. This is the concept that in his plans God included every act of every creature. In his comments on Psalm 139 Gordon H. Clark stated how the Calvinist view of the sovereignty of God works out: "These actions, words, and thoughts had been accurately written down in God's book before any of them took place . . . Every thought and deed had been determined from eternity."[96]

In contrast, God in his gracious providence adjusts and modifies circumstances moment by moment in response to an individual's submission to him or rebellion against him. That is the way I read my

Bible. Scripture presents a far more satisfactory picture of a truly sovereign God who responds to individual human choices; not a picture in which God is limited by having determined every least event and every human response before creation itself.

I am acquainted with all the familiar Calvinist arguments. Foundational arguments were recently expounded by J. R. White in *The Potter's Freedom*. He discussed whether a non-Christian can believe in Christ by a personal decision, or whether a decision to believe is made and carried out by a work of God in the human's heart. If it is by a personal choice rather than by God's choosing, then, according to White, this leads to "the ability of man to control the work of God in salvation and *always* have the 'final say'" [italics his].[97] In other words, if humans have a choice, even in such a matter as believing in Christ, then God's freedom is limited. To limit God's freedom is to make him less than sovereign.

This doctrine certainly seems to make God the author of sin, including the sin of unbelief. The usual rejoinder is that God cannot be the author of sin, since acts of sin are not "prenecessitated." God did not cause sinful acts -- they had "secondary causes"-- but he predestined them. A way it can be put is this: man makes an evil decision, but God concurs in the decision, for the evil decision was God's intention all along. In this view, providence is God not only using but *designing* good and bad, including the most sinful acts, to work out his purposes in the world.

To me, these conclusions are wholly unacceptable, for God appeals to humans to make right decisions, including a decision to be reconciled to him (2 Corinthians 5:20). Is this an empty appeal? Empty it seems it must be, since those on the predestined track will inevitably be reconciled and others simply cannot respond. Jesus said, "Behold, I stand at the door and knock" (Revelation 3:20). Is his knocking a vain enterprise, knowing that the greatest number have never been granted the option of opening? People are commanded to believe in the name of God's Son Jesus Christ (1 John 3:23). Did God ungraciously decide aeons in advance that the great majority of mankind would have no possible chance of believing, because he would deliberately refrain from placing the desire to believe in their hearts? When the Apostle Paul urged Christians to "Pray at all times in the Spirit," and then asked those reading his letter to pray specifically for the success of his ministry (Ephesians 6:18-19), did he think their prayers, even their very words, were predetermined and that the answers were predetermined as well? Answers to prayer are denied those who ask amiss (James 4:3) and who are deaf to the cry of the poor (Proverbs 21:13). Did God intend that some should pray amiss or that some should be deaf to the needs of others? The determinists would answer, "Of course not, but their wrong praying and their deafness was all according to his wise design." Is this true? Are human choices not free? Even though we think they are, is this an illusory appearance?

What do the Scriptures teach? There are numerous passages with a universal appeal, of which Isaiah 45:22 is an example.

Turn to me and be saved,

All the ends of the earth!

For I am God, and there is no other.

Is "all the ends of the earth" an invitation to a limited category? Does "whoever" in John 3:16 mean only a certain class of humans, not really everyone? It reads, "For God so loved the world that he gave his only Son, that whoever believes in him should not perish but have eternal life." In the original Greek the word "world" is *kosmos*. Everywhere else in the Gospel of John, *kosmos* is used of the world of humans. It stands for the world of unregenerate, Christ-rejecting society. (See John 15:18-19.) This is indeed the class whom God loves, the whole unbelieving world, not simply the elect who as a class occupy different places on the globe. All mankind is the class for whom Christ died and to whom God is individually urging reconciliation.

My determinist brethren have an answer. The Scriptures, they say, plainly teach predestination. A clear example is Ephesians 1:4-5, 11-12. Ours is not to question God's revelation, they say, but to make the most of it.

With respect to Ephesians 1:4-5 and 11-12, I need to point out that the interpretation hangs on a correct understanding of Paul's formulaic expression "in Christ" (including "in him," and "in the beloved"). The expression does not mean "by means of Christ" but means "identification with Christ" or "union with Christ."[98] Unquestionably the Scriptures teach that Christ himself was predestined before the foundation of the world (Isaiah 49:7; Acts 2:23; 1 Peter 1:20). What Paul is saying is that when one believes in Christ, that person is united with him and in the sight of God becomes all that Christ is. Christ is predestined. At the point of exercising faith in Christ, a person becomes identified with Christ. Being identified with Christ, along with Christ the believer is predestined to resurrection and to all the other glorious benefits included in salvation.

Among the many predestined-to-faith arguments, one especially needs consideration. If humans are all hopelessly depraved, "dead in trespasses and sins" (Ephesians 2:1-3), and all humans are, then how can one ever make a God-pleasing decision to believe in Christ? It would seem one cannot, for sin never begets good. Yet Jesus taught that God by his Holy Spirit has placed in the mind of everyone (the *kosmos*) a conviction "of sin, of righteousness, and of judgment"

(John 16:8). Of itself the sinful mind could never come to a realization of such facts. But by his sovereign choice God through the Holy Spirit has made it possible for everyone to comprehend, so that anyone hearing the truth as it is in Christ, and believing, may be forgiven and granted eternal life.

I am aware of other Biblical passages that might be cited in defense of the doctrine of determinism. I think the conclusions drawn from them are plain wrong. In the scope of this work these cannot all be analyzed, but in brief the Scriptures teach that *at the point of faith* each one coming to Christ is absolutely predestined to the final, glorious result of God's salvation. (As I read my Bible, this conforms neither to Calvinist nor Arminian constructions!) The offer of salvation is made to all, for at the cross Christ took the penalty that each of us deserves upon himself (1 Peter 2:24). He became our substitute in death, and as a consequence God is able through an act of pure grace to offer forgiveness and eternal life to anyone. That offer can be received by a decision of genuine but simple faith (Ephesians 2:8-9).

One sticky problem requires an answer. If God is in control of every least subatomic event, is he not thereby controlling the mind to make whatever choices it makes? The question defeats everything argued above, *if* we assume that the human mind is nothing more than chemical interactions and neural pathways. Such an explanation of the mind is assumed by the naturalists, but it is an assumption, for no one has explained the human mind. The Christian believes, must indeed believe, that being created in the image of God we are more than mere physical circuitry. If we follow the Scriptures, the Holy Spirit grants all humans the choice to trust God. By the Holy Spirit believers are granted the amazing power to be controlled *not* by their animal natures (the "flesh"), but to choose to follow Christ.

My non-determinist understanding is that God in his sovereignty freely and graciously grants humans what the rest of creation can never experience: genuine moral choices. In his transcendental yet wonderful providence God responds to every decision made by a Christian, whether it be a right or a wrong decision. If the Christian sins, and is unwilling to repent, through providential means God brings loving chastening into that one's life to encourage and point to right choices. God will touch the person where it will best promote the individual's return to him. On the other hand, God responds positively to a committed Christian's prayer. Is someone earnestly seeking an opening to witness of Christ's grace to a scoffing employer? In answer to prayer, God's providence can open a door at the opportune time. Is a young Christian girl honestly seeking God's will regarding a man she hopes to marry? God's providence may lead him to someone else, a disappointment for the girl but safety for her future. The Apostle Paul was stricken with an infirmity, possibly an eye disease. He prayed for relief, but God let him know that the infirmity was to keep him from being filled with pride and to make him realize that his receipt of divine revelations was not his doing but God's grace (2 Corinthians 12:7-9). The point is, providence in a most remarkable way insures that everything works together for the ultimate good of the believer.

God also responds to the unbeliever, yet not as he does to the Christian. He may show goodness with the hope of leading the unbeliever to repentance (Romans 2:4). He may respond to the unbeliever in judgment. God's providence was not cast in concrete from the very beginning, but is flexible. It provides a just and fitting response to every human choice.

Did God know in advance how an individual would respond to him and how he in turn would answer that response? Certainly. But God can know without predetermining every action. Contrary-to-sense modern physics sees time as a fourth dimension of space. We ourselves cannot move back and forth in time as we do in our familiar three dimensions of space. There is no reason, however, why God should not be omnipresent in time just as he is in space. He is present in the future just as much as in the past. In providence, therefore, he can choose moment by moment without predetermining.

The Doctrine of Original Sin

A number of creationist writings insist that the doctrine of original sin is an absolutely critical hinge for creation truth. That may be, but many Christians would have a difficult time explaining just what original sin is supposed to mean. Part of the confusion stems from the fact that within historical Protestantism the doctrine of original sin has taken a number of forms. Exposition of these is unnecessary here, but most Protestant views of original sin look primarily to Romans 5, particularly to verse 12:

> Therefore just as through one man sin entered into the world,
> and death through sin, and so death spread to all men
> because all men sinned –

The Apostle Paul taught that in some way or another every human became chargeable with sin as a consequence of Adam's sin. As the result of that historic act of sin, all mankind must suffer death. Probably the best way to understand the passage is explained by Professor Henri Blocher: "Alienation from God, the condition of being deprived and depraved, follows immediately upon the first act of sinning – for Adam himself and for his seed after him."[99] Human inability to be other than self-centered and to live in autonomy from God began with Adam. There is absolutely no Biblical necessity for thinking that every human became an actual participant in Adam's sin, either by some strange kind of heredity or by a divine fiat.

What has Adam's sin to do with providence? A great deal, because it explains why a God of love looks on rebellious humanity with a most forbidding frown. It also has to do with creation, for it explains why there had to be a literal Adam.

With respect to creation, Christian evolutionary views generally suppose there was an evolving population of humans.[100] It would seem that no evolutionary view, even if it is called Christian, can therefore be true, since Scripturally the human race had to start with one man. If it did not, then the doctrine of original sin falls by the board. It is stretching the language of the Apostle Paul out of all reasonable bounds to suppose he meant that mankind as a class or as a population sinned and passed guilt or disability down to the rest of mankind. (See also Romans 5:17, 19.) If Paul was correct, and I believe he was, then any view of creation that dispenses with a single, literal human father is necessarily defective.

On this score, young-earth creationism, reconstruction creationism and progressive creationism pass muster. All three postulate a single, literal Adam. How have providential creationists treated this problem? Surprisingly, the term "fundamentalist," which today largely stands for Christians who totally reject evolution in favor of young-earth creationism, had its origin in a series of twelve volumes entitled *The Fundamentals*. The volumes, published by the Bible Institute of Los Angeles with a grant from two wealthy oilmen, constituted a defense of Biblical faith. Publication began in 1909, and in 1917 all were republished in their entirety. They were distributed to ministers, missionaries, YMCA's, churches and schools across the country and around the world. In a twist of history, one contributor to *The Fundamentals* was the scholar James Orr, Professor of Apologetics and Systematic Theology in the United Free Church College of Glasgow. Orr was a providential creationist (termed at that time a theistic evolutionist)! In a series of lectures at Princeton Theological Seminary in 1903-4, Dr. Orr expounded his approach to creation. This approach was subsequently published in 1907 as a book entitled *God's Image in Man.*[101] Orr argued that there was a pre-Adamic protohuman race, creatures made through a long process of divinely directed evolution. In a theological sense these were distinguished from modern humans in that they lacked the "image of God." They were human-like in most physical features, but they could not be considered genuinely human. From such an ancestry through a providential macromutation came a literal Adam. The macromutation granted Adam a larger brain capacity. Much more significantly he differed through having been invested with an immaterial spirit. This was the image of God. It was this individual person Adam who walked with God, who consciously sinned, and who brought sin upon all mankind.

Whether we agree with Dr. Orr, at least this much is clear: providential creationism may be formulated in such a way that it comes into no conflict with Paul's teaching in Romans 5 or with the creation passages. For providential creationists, some details of Orr's position need revision in the light of recent discoveries by historical anthropologists. It also seems most unlikely that a macromutation brought Adam into being. Orr was undoubtedly influenced by the investigations of the Dutch botanist Hugo de Vries, whose macromutation theory of evolution had suddenly become popular among biologists. Nevertheless, neither providential creationism nor any of the truly theistic creationist views is necessarily negated by the doctrine of original sin.

Providence and the Mode of Creation

To my knowledge, young-earth, reconstruction, and progressive creationists have never stated whether evolution *below* the level of *kind* (their microevolution) comes about solely through the mechanism of natural selection, or whether it is an operation of providence. Their literature, as far as I have been able to wade through it, seems to assume that microevolution is identical with the natural selection of the biologists.

Herein lies a most interesting difficulty. If God allowed microevolution to produce a number of biological species from an original parent species by *undirected* natural selection, then God has relinquished a measure of his sovereignty. God is not in full control. Random events (random mutations and random environmental changes) are at least in partial control. Most creationist writers seem not to have thought about the matter.[102] In any event, if God's supervision of species formation is in the least part lacking, then by so much his power and sovereignty are diminished. Sovereignty demands that God's providence operate totally.

On the other hand, if in his providential supervision God directs events so that an original biological species evolves into two, three, four, or more species, there is *no theological necessity* why, acting in providence, God cannot have created a hundred or a thousand or ten thousand or a million species from a single ancestral parent! If God in providence can operate to produce two or three biological species out of one, God in providence can also bring about any number of species from an original set of parents. There is no limit to what God can do when in his omniscience and omnipotence he is in control of every least subatomic event. There is no boundary such as, "God must not providentially create a species involving a new family." God can bring about – and surely his power to control events is adequate to the task

– the rise of new genera, new families, new orders, new classes, new phyla and new kingdoms.

The conclusion is this. The doctrine of providence does not prohibit Christians from accepting any of the truly theistic views of creation. It does award a most definite nod to providential creationism, since other views either ignore God's providential power, or if they admit it, they unwittingly remove an important theological barrier to the concept of divinely directed evolution.

What then are the principle conclusions to be drawn from our study? These are briefly stated in the following chapter.

CHAPTER 8

THE EPILOGUE

Before looking at a few conclusions, it may be helpful to comment on some criticisms that I have leveled against certain views, especially against young-earth creationism. In no way has there been an intent to impugn the ability, knowledge, spirit or piety of young-earth advocates. There are leaders in the movement deserving of respect. The Christian must applaud these leaders for their sincere commitment to the Bible as the inerrant Word of God. Nevertheless, their concepts deserve criticism for two reasons. (1) Their widely propagated but totally unnecessary notion of a young earth as true Biblical faith has encouraged many to reject Christ, especially scientists and science students. Their lectures and the dissemination of their literature on university campuses effectively persuade many that Christian faith is tantamount to faith in eighteenth century science. (2) Their want of scientific reasoning fails to provide Christian leaders, parents and teachers accurate information to help guide young people through the welter of religious and secular attacks against sound Biblical faith. The criticisms voiced in the preceding pages are to help Christians retain their faith in a completely inspired Word, without having to deny solidly-based scientific conclusions.

Some readers are likely to object that I have been critical of young-earth creationism without beginning to answer dozens of arguments marshaled against the old earth view and the doctrine of evolution. I readily admit this. As I do, I am reminded of what a few of my readers may have experienced. You walked down a curious kind of street in a California city. It had old-fashioned houses on each side and strange-looking, almost artificial-looking trees. There was no sign of life, no traffic along its cobbled streets. No birds were flying overhead, no faces appeared in the windows. You came to one of the houses about a block and a half down. The door was open, you entered, and behind it you found struts, two-by-fours holding up the wall. It was a façade of a house, a moving picture set on a Hollywood lot. Now you did not have to go back to the other houses to find out that they also were façades. One does not need to minutely examine every argument of young-earth creationists to be convinced that one cannot rely on their teaching when their most fundamental structures are astonishingly empty.

While disagreeing with young-earth creationism, I have no sympathy for the philosophy of evolutionary naturalism, even though I have great respect for the achievements of many evolutionary naturalists and have many friends among them. It must be acknowledged that brilliant minds have built the structure of evolutionary naturalism through inferences from thousands of experiments and observations. To imagine that it will vanish with a few choice objections is wishful thinking. It is here for the duration, for it is the finest intellectual edifice the human mind at enmity with God has yet erected. An effective response to evolutionary naturalism will not come from philosophical reasoning, but will come and can only come as its adherents experience a face-to-face encounter with the Lord of life.

With these preliminary comments, we need to review some basic conclusions.

Conclusion Number 1

Darwinian evolution and providential creationism sit at opposite poles, even though both consider all life to have descended from a common ancestry. Darwinian evolution, the concept espoused by most biologists and paleontologists, holds that God had nothing to do with the course of evolution, that every evolutionary step was fortuitous, unplanned, undesigned and without any goal. Providential creationism holds that God had express designs for life and that every least evolutionary step was under his direct and conscious control. This is the correct definition of intelligent design!

The naturalistic (Darwinian) evolutionist observes natural selection at work and arrives at what is presumably a scientific conclusion: God can have had no hand in the process. There is no explanation needed or possible other than the physical laws of science. Nevertheless, this is a metaphysical conclusion. It is a conclusion assuming that no reality exists except what can be observed by science. Providential creation is also based on a metaphysical conclusion. This conclusion is that the God of the Bible is real, is omnipotent, is omniscient, and works according to his own wise design. The doctrine of providential creation does not deny that natural selection takes place. It considers, however, that behind every mutation and behind every change in the environment is the unseen but real hand of God.

Which doctrine is correct? Can it be settled by an appeal to evidence for intelligent design? Irreducible complexity (the evidence for intelligent design) appears based on careful scientific observation. Nevertheless, even if every evidence of irreducible complexity is ultimately found to have an answer in natural selection, Darwinian evolution will not have triumphed. Its metaphysical roots will remain. Providential creationism, rooted in the metaphysics of Biblical faith, will continue to find its support in the reality of the human condition, and the evidence that humans can experience God and his deliverance from the sin and degradation of this world.

Conclusion Number 2

When the multitude of facts about ancient and existing forms of life are carefully catalogued and compared, evolution seems undeniable. What makes the general concept of evolution highly believable is the *concurrence of a number of independent lines of evidence for the theory*. Each piece of evidence corroborates what is implied by other lines of evidence. Granted, corroboration is not proof, no matter how many independent witnesses get up on the stand. But in the absence of another convincing theory, the lines of evidence make a case that on the basis of every observation is extremely difficult to discount.

Patterns of geographic distribution make sense if a process of evolution is assumed and is *coupled with* the theory of continental drift. The theory of continental drift is powerfully supported by observations of sea-floor spreading, lines of reversed magnetism on the ocean floor, the angles of magnetism in certain minerals on the continents which show that the continents have rotated over time, and radiometric dating showing the increasing ages of ocean-bottom rocks with distance from the midoceanic ridges.

The sequence of fossil forms found in successive strata makes sense assuming an evolutionary process. To be sure, there are gaps in the record. The larger gaps, however, have a random appearance with fewer gaps generally found in more recent rocks. Furthermore, fossils found on the different continents correspond to what would be expected according to the theory of continental drift. Nevertheless, if any line of evidence gives particular credence to progressive creationism it is the existence of a few difficult-to-explain gaps.

Neither the Christian nor the secular world has some theory other than evolution that is capable of putting all the different lines of evidence into a coherent picture. The flood geology view, despite the heroic efforts of its adherents to leap over every obstacle, comes the furthest from succeeding. One cannot help but admire sincere, young-earth creationist attempts to validate the truth of the Bible as they see the truth. As of now they have produced little to convince objective, scientifically-knowledgeable, and even thoroughly Christian observers that they have proposed anything with general explanatory power.

Conclusion No. 3

The issues are far too complex for anyone to assert that one particular theistic view of creation is finally and unquestionably correct, and all others grossly in error. Of the major approaches to which evangelical Christians subscribe, none may be entirely correct and possibly all fall significantly short. Conceivably, a modification of macrotheistic creationism that subscribes to the truth of Scripture may prove valid, even if I cannot see it from my present perspective. Or there may be a surprising new picture just over the horizon waiting for a convincing unveiling.

Because the issues are so complex, it is quite unseemly when some writers castigate every evangelical view but their own as ignorant, unchristian, and a compromise with atheism. Some Christian brethren may entertain mistaken views, but if they give allegiance to the cardinal tenets of our great faith, that faith should be thankfully acknowledged.

Conclusion Number 4

Where can a person turn who has implicit faith in the Word of God, and is earnestly seeking an answer regarding the time and manner of creation? The answer is found in the other book God has left us. This book is the created world with its detailed record of the ages. It has come from God's hand just as much as his written Word. When all the truth is known, the Bible and scientific knowledge will be in perfect accord. This is no less than the Word of God requires.

The Biblical texts do not spell out the time and manner of creation. The Christian student looking for answers need not fear learning from scientists who have spent their lives investigating the earth's biological and geological history, even if many scientists and science teachers are unbelievers. Science has discovered an astounding array of facts regarding the physical universe, and scientists attempt to place the facts together in coherent packages. As new facts are discovered, and as scientists conceive of better explanations, the theories are modified. The student can learn disquieting theories but place them in a tentative file (where all theories belong anyway) and seek better solutions. Most theories are modified over time. Many are discarded and replaced by better ones. Science is not complete. New facts remain to be discovered, and many theories need rethinking. The Christian scientist and science student can have a share in rethinking existing theories. Of course, the student should be aware that some presumed truths touted by some scientists are truths only for those accepting a metaphysical view of the world which out of hand discounts the existence of a personal, all-powerful, infinite God.

Conclusion Number 5

The question of evolution is tangential to the truly important issues of faith. To make the question of creation and evolution central to faith is to miss the whole thrust of Scripture.

The question of how and when creation took place involves an immense body of scientific information. The complexity does not mean an answer is not available or that one has not been found. What it does mean is that a satisfactory answer cannot be given in a short two-day seminar on creation, plus, "You will find books and tapes for sale on the back table!" The question requires thoughtful discussion, an admission of certain large areas of ignorance, gathering of information from a number of scientific fields and, above all, truthfulness that befits servants of the God of truth.

Although questions about creation and evolution may be secondary issues, they need to be answered for people who are honestly perplexed and for whom either misplaced "Christian" pronouncements on science, or the scientisms of some scientists, become stumbling blocks to faith. The Christian who has a knowledge of the issues is doing a service of love to answer or seek answers for anyone who is troubled by seeming impediments to genuine Christian faith, whether from a young person or a professional scientist.

On the other hand, to make the time, place and manner of creation an issue to be debated in public forums before unbelievers, to force textbook publishers to print books sympathetic to a presumably Christian point of view, to seek legislative mandates to force public schools to give equal time to creationism, or to campaign for school board members who will root out of the curriculum the pernicious evil of evolution is to do a terrible disservice to the cause of Christ. Insofar as Satan succeeds in diverting attention from the genuinely critical issues of our faith, he has won a tremendous victory. When he can sidetrack the faithful into spending their time and money on secondary issues (and the time and method of God's creative work is a secondary issue) he has succeeded in diluting propagation of truth that counts.

"Intelligent design" is the new watchword of many Christian anti-evolutionists. Hence some school boards made up of Christians are insisting that intelligent design (or irreducible complexity) be added to the biology curriculum of schools as an alternative to evolution. As usually presented, this is a disservice to both Biblical faith and an understanding of the history of biology. Intelligent design is not an anti-evolution argument. It is an argument against unaided, undirected, wholly random natural selection as the total explanation of evolution.

I am not suggesting that school boards remove from the high school biology curriculum any reference to intelligent design or even to young-earth creation theory. It is a disservice to teachers (and I think an illegal activity) when boards or administrators censure or dismiss a teacher for mentioning intelligent design as an alternative to unaided, non-directional natural selection. Sound education requires that students encounter and think through major competing theories of any controversial subject. The origin of life and the concept of evolution are controversial, even if most professional biologists are free of any lingering doubts. Students presented with different sides of an issue will experience an increased interest in the subject, and are more likely to learn essential material than if they are presented cold, disinterested, matter-of-fact, these-you-must-remember details. The voting Christian can well make an effort to cast his or her ballot for informed and thoughtful school board members who can help shape integrated and challenging curricula that allow consideration of conflicting ideas. This is, however, quite different from making any sort of creationist doctrine a public issue.

During the school semesters of 1938-39 I was attending a graduate school in Philadelphia. During that time the Rev. J. Frank Norris, a prominent Fort Worth preacher and renowned fundamentalist, came to the city for a short evangelistic campaign. Advertisements of the meetings were placarded on subway trains and billboards throughout the entire metropolitan area. Along with an enormous crowd, I attended the first meeting. But this sad preacher spent his entire time decrying the communist tendencies of the government and the particular pink tint of First Lady Eleanor Roosevelt. I am sure he thought people needed to be warned about the direction in which American politics was moving. Sadly the gospel was conspicuously absent, and no one was reconciled to God and found forgiveness and eternal life in Christ. We can cluck our tongues at the misplaced priorities of this Baptist evangelist and admit that Satan turned the meeting to hell's advantage. Just as much, however, Satan wrests our Christian priorities when he makes evolution versus creation the all-consuming preoccupation of any believer.

What should be the consuming passion of those who know the Lord of grace? The Apostle Paul wrote to the Corinthians, "For I decided to know nothing among you except Jesus Christ and him crucified" (1 Corinthians 2:2). There were many problems in Corinth that needed solving. The social institution of slavery was one. The cruelty and often unjust jurisprudence of the Romans was another. Yet Paul did not address these or other concerns, even though they may have had some secondary values for the community of the faithful. Paul kept his focus on what was truly essential. The very center of his focus was that the embodied Son of God suffered death on the cross in place of sinners, so that God in grace might provide forgiveness and eternal life to all willing to place their faith in Jesus Christ and his resurrection from the dead. With the help of God, that essential message is mine and should be the message of every Christian.

INDEX

NOTES

1. George E. Webb, "Tucson's Evolution Debate, 1924-1927," *Jour. Arizona History*, Spring, 1983: 1-12.

2.(Green Forest, AR: Master Books, 2003)

3. Darwin's intent to show that evolution occurred through natural laws apart from the interposition of divine power is nicely explained by John Angus Campbell in his chapter, "Intelligent Design, Darwinism, and the Philosophy of Public Education," John Angus Campbell and Stephen C. Meyer, ed., *Darwinism, Design, and Public Education* (East Lansing: Michigan State Univ. Press, 2003), 3-44.

4. What is valid science? Not all philosophers of science are agreed. See a fascinating dialog between a positivist, a relativist, a pragmatist and a realist in Larry Laudan, *Science and Relativism: Some Key Controversies in the Philosophy of Science* (Chicago: Univ. of Chicago Press, 1990). I believe the four realist principles listed on p. 59 are valid, for this is the way the science I know operates.

5. Michael Roberts, "The Genesis of Ray and His Successors or the Fall of the House of Ussher," *Evangelical Quarterly*, April (2002):225-55.

6. Recent young-earth creationists leaders do not think that a canopy contributed substantially to global flood waters, if at all.

7. More than any other work, young earth creationism was popularized for the evangelical public by John C. Whitcomb and Henry M. Morris in their book, *The Genesis Flood: The Biblical Record and Its Scientific Implications* (Philadelphia: Presbyterian and Reformed Publ., 1961). Morris has vigorously defended the view in a number of subsequently published books. An elegant history of the interpretation is found in Ronald L. Numbers, *The*

Creationists: The Evolution of Scientific Creationism (New York: Knopf, 1992). A thoughtful, philosophical defense of the position is Paul Nelson and John Mark Reynolds, "Young Earth Creationism" in J. P. Moreland and John Mark Reynolds, *Three Views on Creation and Evolution* (Grand Rapids: Zondervan, 1999).

8. Those concerned that the Bible teaches a world-wide flood should read the excellent analysis by Davis A. Young, *The Biblical Flood: A Case Study of the Church's Response to Extrabiblical Evidence* (Grand Rapids: Eerdmans, 1995).

9. Gregory P. Elder, *Chronic Vigour: Darwin, Anglicans, Catholics, and the Development of a Doctrine of Providential Evolution* (Lanham, MD: Univ. Press of America, 1996), 85-120.

10. A modern view of providential creationism is found in Gordon C. Mills, "A Theory of Theistic Evolution as an Alternative to the Naturalistic Theory" (*Perspectives on Science and Christian Faith*, 47 (1995): 112-22), and Mills, "Similarities and Differences in Mitochondrial Genomes: Theistic Interpretations," Ibid. 50 (1998): 286-291. As Mills approaches the problems he allows chance a greater role than I think is necessary.

11. Hans Küng, *Does God Exist? An Answer for Today*, trans. Edward Quinn (Garden City: Doubleday, 1978), 645.

12. Was Charles Darwin a macrotheistic creationist? Darwin accounted for the existence of matter and life through a Creator. He did not specify what that Creator was. The Princeton Seminary theologian Charles Hodge analyzed the *Origin of Species* and concluded that Darwin must have been an atheist. Asa Gray, the famous Harvard botanist, a Christian friend of Hodge and a correspondent of Darwin's, read Darwin differently. For an interesting debate, see Nark A. Noll and David N. Livingstone, ed., *Charles Hodge: What is Darwinism? And Other Writings on Science and Religion* (Grand Rapids: Baker Books, 1994).

13. John Polkinghorne, *Belief in God in an Age of Science* (New Haven: Yale, 1998), 13-4.

14. Howard J. Van Till, "Special Creation in Designer Clothing." *Perspectives on Science and Christian Faith* 47, no. 2 (1995):124. Also see expositions of his view in Van Till, *The Fourth Day* (Grand Rapids: Eerdmans, 1986); and Van Till, "The Fully Gifted Creation" *in* J. P. Moreland and John Mark Reynolds, *Three Views on Creation and Evolution* (Grand Rapids: Zondervan, 1999), 159-218.

15. Mutations combined with environmental change are considered two essential factors in evolution, but to produce separate species, most biologists consider some form of isolation is required. A few biologists think species can also be produced by something termed sympatric speciation, but the concept has been difficult to demonstrate.

16. For a fascinating account of the way a modern geneticist uses mathematical probabilities to account for the differences in percentages of the genetic disease termed *complete imperfect albinism,* a disease among various human populations that ranges from 1 in 36,000 among European-Americans in the United States to 1 in 192 among the Zuni Indians of New Mexico, see Charles M. Woolf, "Albinism (OCA2) in Amerindians," *Yearbook of Physical Anthropology* 48(2006):118-140.

17. Richard Dawkins, *The Blind Watchmaker* (New York: W. W. Norton, 1987), 5.

18."Darwin's Influence on Modern Thought," *Scientific American* Jul, 283 (2000):78-83.

19. There are scholars who believe that Gen. 1 does not teach that God created the universe out of nothing but began with a preexisting formless material. Their views are competently answered in Paul Copan and William Lane Craig in "Craftsman or

Creator? An Examination of the Mormon Doctrine of Creation and a Defense of *Creatio ex nihilo,*" Francis J. Beckwith, Carl Mosser, and Paul Owen, ed., *The New Mormon Challenge* (Grand Rapids: Zondervan, 2002), 95-152. It is surprising that the NAB, an approved Roman Catholic version, translates verses 1-2, "In the beginning, when God created the heavens and the earth, the earth was a formless wasteland, and darkness covered the abyss, while a mighty wind swept over the waters." The implication is that God began his creative work with a preexisting formless wasteland. Perhaps it is less surprising that the NRSV adopts essentially the same erroneous translation.

[20]. Source critics of Genesis consider the chapter to have received its final form during or shortly after the Exile, since, according to the Wellhausen hypothesis, it is a "Priestly" document. For a contrary view, among others, U. Cassuto, *A Commentary on the Book of Genesis: Part I, from Adam to Noah*, trans. Israel Abrahams (Jerusalem: Magnes Press, 1961), may be consulted. See his bibliography, 18-9. One cannot help but applaud the conclusion of Dr. J. H. Hertz, Late Chief Rabbi of the British Empire, writing in *The Pentateuch and Haftorahs* (London: Soncino Press, 1960), vii: "My conviction that the criticism of the Pentateuch associated with the name of Wellhausen is a perversion of history and a desecration of religion, is unshaken; likewise my refusal to eliminate the Divine either from history or from human life."

[21]. Bruce K. Waltke, *Creation and Chaos: an Exegetical and Theological Study of Biblical Cosmogony* (Portland: Western Conservative Baptist Seminary, 1974) sees Gen. 1:1-2 as a polemic against the gods of foreign kingdoms. If Gen. 1 had an early origin, these verses may have been directed against Sumerian religious influences. Claus Westerman, *Creation* (Philadelphia: Fortress, 1974) also sees it as an ancient document which may have been a protest against Sumerian religion. We cannot know for sure against whom it is a protest without knowing the date of its composition, and that is still an obscure matter. Each element of Chapter 1, however, fits as a refutation of Egyptian cosmogony.

The list of Egyptian deities, their histories, and their functions is extensive and involved. For detailed accounts consult Byron E. Shafer, ed., *Religion in Ancient Egypt* (Ithaca: Cornell Univ., 1991).

[22]. Gerhard von Rad, *Genesis, A Commentary*, trans. John H. Marks on the basis of 9th German ed. (Philadelphia: Westminster, 1972), 61.

[23]. Gordon J. Wenham, *Genesis 1-15*. Word Biblical Commentary, vol. 1 (Waco: Word Books, 1987), 29-32.

[24]. von Rad, *Genesis*, 59.

[25]. Walter Brueggemann, *Genesis: In Bible Commentary for Teaching and Preaching* (Atlanta: John Knox Press, 1982), 22-5, considers the structure nonetheless poetic designed during the exile for liturgical use as a refutation of Babylonian theological claims.

[26]. von Rad, *Genesis*, 40. Interesting support for this position from modern physics is found in an article by the German physicist Peter Zoeller-Greer, "Genesis, quantum physics, and reality - an anthropic principle of another kind; the Divine anthropic principle." *Perspectives on Science and Christian Faith* 52, no. 1 (2000): 8-17.

[27]. Henry M. Morris, *The Genesis Record* (Grand Rapids: Baker, 1976), 55-56.

[28]. E. H. Andrews, "The Biblical and Philosophical Case for Special Creation" *in* Derek Burke, ed., *Creation and Evolution* (Leicester: Intervarsity, 1985), 226-52.

[29]. Davis A. Young, *Creation and the Flood: An Alternative to Flood Geology and Theistic Evolution* (Grand Rapids: Baker, 1977)

30. Hugh Ross, *The Fingerprint of God* (Orange: Promise Publ., 1991).

31. Bernard Ramm, *The Christian View of Science and Scripture* (Buffalo: Prometheus, 1954), 196, n. 26, summarizes the history of the interpretation, which goes back to Edgar, King of England, in the tenth century.

32. Arthur C. Custance, *Without Form and Void* (Brockville, Ontario, 1970).

33. John Sailhamer, *Genesis Unbound* (Sisters, OR: Multnomah Books, 1996).

34. Frederick Hugh Capron, *The Conflict of Truth* (London: Hodder & Stoughton, 1903).

35. R. C. Newman and Herman J. Ecklemann, Jr., *Genesis One and the Origin of the Earth* (Downers Grove: Intervarsity, 1977).

36. P. J. Wiseman, *Creation Revealed in Six Days* (London: Morgan and Scott, 1948).

37. Henri Blocher, *In the Beginning,* transl. David G. Preston (Downers Grove: Intervarsity, 1984).

38. Augustus H. Strong, *Systematic Theology: A Compendium and Commonplace-book Designed for the Use of Theological Students* (Philadelphia: Judson Press, 1906).

39. "Framework interpretation" is the designation given and developed by W. Robert Godfrey, *God's Pattern for Creation: A Covenantal Reading of Genesis 1* (Phillipsburg, NJ: P&R Publishing Co., 2003).

40. E. W. Bullinger, *Figures of Speech Used in the Bible: Explained and Illustrated* (London: Eyre & Spottiswoode, 1898), 368.

41. Cassuto, 28-30. See the same argument in David A. Sterchi, "Does Genesis 1 Provide a Chronological Sequence?" *Jour. Evangelical Theol. Soc.* 39, no. 4 (1996): 529-536.

42. C. F. Keil and F. Delitzsch, *The Pentateuch*. vol. 1, trans. James Martin. Biblical Commentary on the Old Testament. (Grand Rapids: Eerdmans, 1951), 50-52. E. J. Young sought to refute the thematic interpretation, which he designated the "framework hypothesis" in his *Studies in Genesis One* (Philadelphia: Presbyterian & Reformed Publ., 1964), 43-76.

43. Personal communication.

44. David A. Dorsey, *The Literary Structure of the Old Testament: A Commentary on Genesis – Malachi* (Grand Rapids: Baker, 1999), 20.

45. Cassuto, *From Adam to Noah*, 134.

46. The Hebrew scholar Meridith G. Kline, "Because It Had Not Rained," *Westminster Theol. Jour.*, 20, no. 2 (1958): 146-157, argued for a thematic understanding of Genesis 1 but took a stimulating approach which puts Genesis 1, 2, and 3 in essentially the same genre. He proposed that Gen. 1 looks at creation from a heavenly ("upper register") perspective. Gen. 2-3 sees creation from an earthly ("lower register") perspective. Gen. 2:3 is a transition recording the institution of the lower level phenomenon.

47. Russell Maatman, *The Impact of Evolutionary Theory: A Christian View* (Sioux Center: Dordt College, 1993).

48. Wenham, *Genesis*, 50. Wenham credits P. Auffret with discovery of the structure. The same chiastic structure is nicely illustrated by Sidney Greidanus in "Preaching Christ from the

---

Narrative of the Fall," *Bibliotheca Sacra* 161, no. 643 (2004):259-73. Dorsey, *Literary Structure*, 50, finds a chiastic structure in the passage, but divides the verses somewhat differently than exhibited here.

49. Many different interpretations of the tree have been proposed. Wenham, *op. cit.*, or other commentators should be consulted for a discussion of solutions other than the one outlined here.

50. Claude Tresmontant, *Etudes de métaphysique biblique* (Paris: Gabalda, 1955), 143.

51. It might be argued that Hebrew writers of that early age knew nothing of apocalyptic writing, and so it is highly unlikely that such a genre as "retrospective apocalypse" ever existed a thousand years before Christ. This overlooks the fact that the highly-structured narrative is unique to begin with. It also overlooks the possibility that God's Spirit could well have prompted such writing in the mind of a person in any age of time.

52. For example, J. C. Whitcomb, *The Early Earth* (Grand Rapids, MI: Baker, 1972).

53. See the useful discussion of various possible interpretations in Gordon D. Fee, *The First Epistle to the Corinthians,* The New International Commentary on the New Testament, ed. F. F. Bruce (Grand Rapids: Eerdmans, 1987), 512-30.

54. Douglas J. Moo, *The Epistle to the Romans*, New International Commentary on the New Testament, ed. Gordon D. Fee (Eerdmans: Grand Rapids, 1996), 513.

55. Walter Bauer, *A Greek-English Lexicon of the New Testament and Other Early Christian Literature*, 4th revised and augmented edition by William F. Arndt and F. Wilbur Gingrich (Chicago: Univ. Chicago, 1952).

56. A summary discussion of the entire passage in Moo, *Romans,*

508-10 is most helpful, as are his more detailed notes that follow.

57. Even the very cautious, young-earth, creationist writers Wayne Friar and Percival Davis have accepted this kind of reasoning in their *Case for Creation,* 3d rev. ed. (Lewisville, TX: Accelerated Christian Education, 1983)

58. Steven A. Austin, "Interpreting Strata of the Grand Canyon" *in* Steven A. Austin, ed., *Grand Canyon: Monument to Catastrophe* (Santee, CA: Institute for Creation Research 1994), 21-56.

59. Austin, *Grand Canyon*, 26-8. Stanley S. Beus, paleontologist and respected investigator of the Redwall, informed me that this is not really accurate.

60. An interesting article on conodont teeth and the creatures bearing them is Mark A. Purnell, "Microwear on conodont elements and macrophagy in the first vertebrates," *Nature* 374, no. 6525 (1995): 798-800.

61. Stanley S. Beus, "Redwall Limestone and Surprise Canyon Formation" in *Grand Canyon Geology*, Stanley S. Beus and Michael Morales, ed. (New York: Oxford Univ. Press, 1990), 119-145.

62. Ronald Blakey, "Supai Group and Hermit Formation" in Beus and Morales, ed., *Grand Canyon*, 147-182.

63. Larry T. Middleton, David K. Elliot, and Michael Morales, "Coconino Sandstone" in Beus and Morales, ed., *Grand Canyon,*183-202

64. Alfred S. Romer, *Vertebrate Paleontology*, 2d ed. (Chicago: Univ. Chicago, 1945), 475-484.

65. Kurt P. Wise, "The Origin of Life's Major Groups," *in* J. P. Moreland, ed., *The Creation Hypothesis* (Downer's Grove: InterVarsity, 1994), 211-234.

66. Stephen J. Gould, *Eight Little Piggies* (New York: Norton, 1993), 342-352.

67. Per Brinck, "Onychophora," in Bertil Hanström, Per Brinck, and Gustaf Rudebeck, *South African Animal Life* (Stockholm: Almqvist & Wiksell, 1955), 4:7-31.

68. See a summary of the current hypothesis explaining magnetic pole reversals in Gary A. Glatzmaier and Peter Olson, "Probing the Geodynamo," *Scientific American* 292 (4) (2005):51-57.

69. In scientific notation, uranium-235 is represented as ^{235}U.

70. Zircons themselves may be contaminated with small amounts of other minerals allowing some of the lead to leach out. When analyzed this would lead to an older than actual date. A method has been devised that provides consistent results eliminating the effect of lead loss. Roland Mundil et al., "Age and Timing of the Permian Mass Extinctions: U/Pb Dating of Closed-system Zircons," *Science* 305, No. 5691 (17 Sept., 2004): 1760-3.

71. Anyone interested in a history of the successful struggle to achieve accurate potassium/argon dating should read the fascinating account by William Glen, *The Road to Jaramillo: Critical Years of the Revolution in Earth Science* (Stanford: Stanford Univ., 1982).

72. An interesting dating method is the argon-argon dating technique, too complex to be described here, but widely used today and useful in confirming other dating techniques.

73. Henry M. Morris, *The Biblical Basis for Modern Science* (Grand Rapids: Baker Book House, 1984).

74. Romer, *Vertebrate Paleontology*, 227-8, 247-54.

75. George F. Howe listed a number of plant forms that seem to

appear in the rocks out of their expected order in "Paleobotanical Evidences for a Philosophy of Creationism," *Creation Research Soc.*, 1964 Annual, 24-29. His examples are interesting and refreshing compared with much flood geology writing. It might be noted that he culled his examples from paleobotanical literature where they are described as anomalies needing study rather than as serious exceptions.

76. Duane T. Gish, "Creation, Evolution, and the Historical Evidence," *Amer. Biology Teacher*, 1973:132-140

77. Donald R. Prothero and Robert M. Schock, ed., *The Evolution of the Perissodactyls* (New York: Oxford Univ., 1989).

78. Niles Eldredge, "An Extravagance of Species," *Natural History* 89, no.7 (1980): 46-51.

79.Darrel R. Falk, an evangelical Christian, has written an excellent book, *Coming to Peace with Science: Bridging the Worlds Between Faith and Biology* (Downers Grove: Intervarsity Press, 2004), in which he describes many transitional forms once considered unbridgeable gaps. He includes a convincing discussion on why scientists can't find more transitional forms. See particularly pages 81-134.

80. A nicely written explanation for the non-scientist of current theories for a naturalistic origin of life is Massimo Pigliucci, "Where Do We Come From? A Humbling Look at the Biology of Life's Origin," *in* Campbell and Meyer, *Darwinism, Design, and Public Education*, 193-206.

81. Charles B. Thaxton, Walter L. Bradley, and Roger L. Olsen, *The Mystery of Life's Origin: Reassessing Current Theories* (New York: Philosophical Library, 1984). The interested reader might also consult the chapter, "Attack and Counterattack: The Science of Thermodynamics" in the book by young-earth creationist Duane T. Gish, *Creation Scientists Answer Their Critics*, (El Cajon, CA: Institute for Creation Research, 1993), 151-208. He demonstrates

in good detail why the Second Law of Thermodynamics forbids any assemblage of organic molecules randomly coming together to produce even the simplest conceivable living organism. Someone reading Gish should beware, however, because at the end of his chapter (205) he jumps illogically from thermodynamics and the origin of life to the totally separate and unexplained conclusion that thermodynamics positively forbids the evolution of an initial form of life evolving into the complex forms we know today.

[82]. Michael J. Behe, *Darwin's Black Box: the Biochemical Challenge to Evolution* (New York: The Free Press, 1996)

[83]. Kenneth R. Miller, *Finding Darwin's God* (New York: Cliff Street Books, 1999).

[84]. Michael J. Behe, "Answering Scientific Criticisms of Intelligent Design" in Michael J. Behe, William A. Dembski, and Stephen C. Meyer, *Science and Evidence for Design in the Universe*, Wethersfield Institute Proceedings, 1999 (San Francisco: Ignatius, 2000), 133-49.

[85].Snodgrass, R. E., *Principles of Insect Morphology* (New York: McGraw-Hill, 1935), 586-592.

[86]. Jacques Carayon, 1966. "Traumatic Insemination and the Paragenital System," in R. L. Usinger, *Monograph of Cimicidae* (College Park: Entomological Society of America), 81-166.

[87]. William G. Eberhard, *Sexual Selection and Animal Genitalia* (Cambridge, MA: Harvard U. Press, 1985), 95.

[88]. R. E. Snodgrass, *The Anatomical Life of the Mosquito* (Washington, DC: Smithsonian Institution, 1959), 76.

[89]. For reasons that follow from the understanding of providence that I develop, I see no need to distinguish between general providence and special providence.

90. An account of ways various thinkers have proposed that God intervenes in nature is found in Philip D. Clayton, *God and Contemporary Science* (Grand Rapids: Eerdmans, 1997), 197-227.

91. The physicist William G. Pollard in his book *Chance and Providence*, rev. ed. (New York, Scribner's, 1958) has a fine treatment of this view of providence and as well of some other proposed explanations of providence. Peter van Inwagen has treated the problem of chance differently than I have and probably more thoughtfully. Those troubled with the problem should read his excellent essay, "Doubts about Darwinism," *in* John Buell and Virginia Hearn, ed., *Darwinism, Scientific Inference or Philosophical Preference?* (Richardson, TX: Foundation for Thought and Ethics), 107-113. For an historical review of the way theologians have sought to relate God to the physical world, see Ian Barbour, *Religion in an Age of Science* (San Francisco: Harper and Rowe, 1990-91), 1:243-70. A neo-Thomistic view is proposed by Elizabeth A. Johnson, C.S.J., "Does God Play Dice? Divine Providence and Chance" *in* James B. Miller, ed., *An Evolving Dialogue: Theological and Scientific Perspectives on Evolution* (Harrisburg, PA: Trinity Press International, 2001), 353-70.

92. Kantorovich, Aharon, *Scientific Discovery: Logic and Tinkering* (Albany: State Univ. of New York, 1993), 59.

93. Letter of May 22, 1860.

94. Edward O. Wilson, *The Diversity of Life* (Cambridge: Belknap, 1992).

95. Atheistic opponents have written numerous books seeking to undermine theism by claiming that belief in a loving, personal, and all-powerful God is incompatible with the widespread suffering and death of innocents. Christian apologists have answered from different perspectives. A nice statement of various apologetic approaches is found in Stephen B. Cowan, *Five Views on Apologetics* (Grand Rapids: Zondervan, 2000).

[96]. Gordon H. Clark, *Predestination* (Phillipsburg: Presbyterian and Reformed, 1987), 177.

[97]. J. R. White, *The Potter's Freedom: A Defense of the Reformation and a Rebuttal of Norman Geisler's Chosen But Free* (Amityville, NY: Calvary Press, 2000), 85

[98]. Ever since 1892, when Adolph Deismann published his detailed studies of the formula, there has been controversy among scholars regarding its precise meaning. For those acquainted with Greek, possibly the best analysis is still that of J. O. F. Murray in *The Epistle of Paul to the Ephesians* in *Cambridge Greek Testament for Schools and Colleges* (Cambridge: Cambridge Univ. Press, 1914), lxii-lxxvi. Recently F. F. Bruce concurred with earlier scholars, defining it as "union with him" in *Epistles to the Colossians, to Philemon, and to the Ephesians* (Grand Rapids: Eerdmans, 1984), 254. So also J. D. G. Dunn in *The Epistles to Colossians and Philemon: a Commentary on the Greek Text* in *New International Greek Testament Commentary* (Grand Rapids: Eerdmans, 1996), 49-50.

[99]. Henri Blocher, *Original Sin: Illuminating the Riddle* (Grand Rapids: Eerdmans, 1999), 128.

[100]. For the most part it is theologians of theologically liberal persuasion who interpret Adam as symbolic of a population of humans or as representative of mankind generally. A recent study holding to the authority of Scripture and yet taking Adam to represent either "everyperson" or a group of ancient hominids who had the capacity for free choice and self consciousness is Robin Collins, "Evolution and Original Sin" *in* Keith B. Miller, ed., *Perspectives on an Evolving Creation* (Grand Rapids: Eerdmans, 2003), 469-501. In my estimation, Collins's interpretation of Gen. 1-3 as "mythic" is unnecessary and quite unlikely in view of the carefully crafted literary structures of the chapters. Mythic creation stories of other cultures have none of the precise and thoughtful language of Gen. 1-3. Collins believes that Rom. 5 can

be understood with Adam representing "everyman" as well as an original group of hominids. He recognizes that Paul no doubt thought of Adam as a literal person, but in the light of modern science he thinks it is possible to structure Paul's argument in this way and not do violence to his concept of original sin. The view employs what seems to me a deficient concept of Biblical inspiration.

101. Orr, *God's Image in Man and Its Defacement in the Light of Modern Denials* (Grand Rapids: Eerdmans, reprint of 1905 publ., 1948).

102. Perhaps it is not surprising that Darwin thought about the problem. In *The Variation of Animals and Plants under Domestication* (London: J. Murray, 1871), 2:515-6, he noted that animal breeders might produce a dog of "indomitable ferocity . . . for man's brutal sport." He asked whether God produced the variations that allow such a breed to be developed. Darwin expected his readers to answer No. This being agreed to, it follows that other variations can have come into existence without the direction of God. At what point then can anyone reasonably argue that God designed any of the variations leading to the great succession of evolutionary steps? Darwin's argument was that God could not be present in evolution unless we grant that he is responsible for evil as well as benign traits in organisms.

Made in the USA
Lexington, KY
01 November 2010